HONEST RELIGION
FOR SECULAR MAN

It's so easy to blame God for the mischief of life. A man dies on the operating table. We scream at God. What we don't know is that the surgeon cheated on his exams. He thot he could get by -- but life's not that way. (Tho I'm sure a doctor can't get by ..)

Why scream if there be no God? It's only man's failure. But — you say — human life is valueable. If there be no God human life has no value .. in fact it is a liability to be rid of. Consult your civilizations. Life only has value if we're responsible to a Supreme Lord for it. —Else its only fear for our own similar treatment.

A life in genuine worldliness is possible only through the proclamation of Christ crucified.

Dietrich Bonhoeffer

Honest Religion
for
Secular Man

by
LESSLIE NEWBIGIN

THE WESTMINSTER PRESS
Philadelphia

LIBRARY OF CONGRESS CATALOG CARD NO. 66–16552

Published by The Westminster Press®
Philadelphia, Pennsylvania

PRINTED IN THE UNITED STATES OF AMERICA

CONTENTS

INTRODUCTION

THE following pages reproduce, with some changes, the substance of what was given as the Firth Lectures in the University of Nottingham last November 1964. Some changes and rearrangements have been made, and the last chapter has been entirely rewritten. I am deeply grateful to Dr Hallward, then Vice-Chancellor of the University, and to his colleagues, both for the invitation to give these lectures, and for the great kindness and hospitality which made the visit a very happy and memorable experience. I am grateful also to a number of friends who have read and criticized the lectures, especially to the Reverend David Edwards, Dr Paul Löffler, Dr Terence Tice and Dr Charles West. All of these have been generous in giving time to helping me to remove the defects of the first draft. I am grateful also to Miss G. I. Mather who rendered the whole of my confused and illegible screed into lucid type upon which it was possible for others to comment.

The Firth Lecturer is invited to speak to the members of the University on some matter connected with the interpretation of the Christian Faith. I decided to attempt some discussion of an issue which many have treated much more competently than I can do, but which no Christian living in the modern world can evade. If there is any justification for adding one more book to the number already available on the secular interpretation of the Gospel it is that, as I hope, the experience of working for twenty-three years as a missionary in India and for five years in the International Missionary Council and the World Council of Churches may provide an angle of vision which can enable some things to be seen more clearly than from a purely western point of view.

Since the two key words of my title are the words 'religion' and 'secular' it might seem necessary to begin with a definition of them. I must ask to be excused from doing this, for the whole argument of the book will be concerned to show what I believe to be the proper content of these two words. But let me at least try to avoid unnecessary misunderstanding by making an essential distinction. During the present discussion, the words 'secular' and 'secularization' will be used in a sense which is not the same as 'secularist' and 'the propagation or spread of secularism'. I take 'secularism' to refer to a system of belief, or an attitude, which in principle denies the existence or the significance of realities other than those which can be measured by the methods of natural science. It was defined at the Jerusalem meeting of the International Missionary Council (1928) as 'a way of life and an interpretation of life that include only the natural order of things and that do not find God, or a realm of spiritual reality, necessary for life or thought'.[1] For the purposes of the present discussion I am making a distinction which was not made at the Jerusalem meeting between 'secularism' as a closed system of belief and 'secularization' which is a historical process of which the writer and his readers are a part. This process may be looked at both in its negative and in its positive aspects. Negatively, it is the withdrawal of areas of life and activity from the control of organized religious bodies, and the withdrawal of areas of thought from the control of what are believed to be revealed religious truths. Positively it may be seen as the increasing assertion of the competence of human science and technics to handle human problems of every kind. In a biblical perspective (as will be argued) this can be seen as man's entering into the freedom given to him in Christ, freedom from the control of all other powers, freedom for

[1] International Missionary Council, *Jerusalem Meeting Report*, Vol. I, p. 284.

the mastery of the created world which was promised to man according to the Bible. At its best the secular spirit claims the freedom to deal with every man simply as man and not as the adherent of one religion or another, and to use all man's mastery over nature to serve the real needs of man. At the Jerusalem meeting Dr John Mackay said: 'In many of its aspects, secular civilization is the disinterested pursuit of human welfare', and this positive evaluation of the secular has won increasing recognition among Christians. That it does not necessarily carry with it the implication of a denial of all reality to the claims of religion is illustrated in the following sentence of the 1951 Election Manifesto of the Indian Congress Party: 'As India is a secular state, every citizen has the same duties, rights, privileges and obligations. He has full freedom to profess and practise his religion.'

The words 'secular' and 'religious' are normally contraries. Christianity has been traditionally interpreted as part of the world of religion. The present discussion questions the tradition – and with justice. The attack upon 'religion' in the name of the Gospel, launched with such power by Karl Barth and further developed by Dietrich Bonhoeffer, contains, I believe, a large element of truth. I happen to have spent most of my working life in two cities dominated by famous temples and dedicated to the propagation of religion on a massive scale. I have seen enough to know how powerful a source of evil religion can be. Nor is it necessary to go outside Europe to have that demonstration. In one sense the Gospel is indeed the end of religion. The penetrating and yet tantalizing paragraphs in which Bonhoeffer, near the end of his life, spoke of man's coming of age and sketched the outlines for a 'religionless' Christianity are among the most powerful formative influences in the life of the Church today. Nevertheless, I do not believe that truth is served by joining in the general chant: 'Up with the secular: down with religion.' Much more careful thinking is needed. Religion is much too great and permanent an element in human experience to be swept out of sight. The

Gospel is the end of religion, as it is the end of the law. But law remains a reality in the life of a Christian, and so, I am persuaded, is religion. I want in these lectures to ask what must be the religion of a Christian who accepts the process of secularization and lives fully in the kind of world into which God has led us.

I have used the phrase 'Honest Religion'. I have in mind not only the famous book of the Bishop of Woolwich, but much more the less well-known book of the man who was my teacher of theology, John Oman. In giving to one of his books the title *Honest Religion* he was giving expression to something very characteristic of his whole theology. He was more aware than many theologians are of the ease with which theology can become dishonest. He insisted on asking at every point the question: 'How do you know?' It is one of the accidents of history that his greatest book, *The Natural and the Supernatural*, a superb intellectual achievement by a profoundly honest thinker, appeared just at the time when the rise of the Barthian theology was sweeping that question under the carpet. I have a feeling, perhaps wrongly, that too many churchmen in Britain were glad to see that happen, without being ready to face with full seriousness the other questions which Karl Barth put to them. But now, whatever we may have done or failed to do with Barth, we are facing again the questions to which John Oman devoted his tremendous intellectual powers. I hope I am not such a fool as to compare myself with him in respect of competence to discuss these questions. But I would like to think of these lectures as something of a tribute from a former pupil, and to express the hope that they may reflect something of the honesty with which he wrestled with these questions.

1

THE PROCESS OF SECULARIZATION

Secularization as a Universal Fact

T H E most significant fact about the time in which we are
living is that it is a time in which a single movement of
secularization is bringing the peoples of all continents into
its sweep. So large a generalization will obviously call for
qualifications in detail, but I hope to be allowed to take it
as our starting-point. Let me speak for a moment of the two
aspects under which one may regard this single movement
– as unification, and as secularization.

Jet-propelled travel and radio communication have put
every part of the world into immediate contact with every
other. As a result more and more people read the same news, *or world*
share the same ideas, worry about the same problems,
dream the same dreams. In almost every country it is possible to buy a local newspaper and read the important world
news of yesterday. In small villages of Asia and Africa
people who cannot read or write sit around the common
radio to hear what has been said in New York, Moscow,
Paris – or even London. In cities such as Geneva a cosmopolitan society of diplomats and civil servants, drawn from
every country and every culture, constitutes a perpetual
informal parliament of ideas. The universities of almost
every country are cosmopolitan in composition, certainly as
far as concerns the student body and increasingly also in the
teaching staff. It is true that there are still large parts of the
earth where society continues with very little change, as, for
example, in immense stretches of the Amazon basin, in
Tibet, in the highlands of New Guinea. But these areas
represent only the stragglers in the march. In every country

the direction and the pace of human life are set by the big cities, and these constitute now a single network of inter-dependent thought and activity, linked together by innumer-able commercial, political and cultural relationships, so that a movement in any part immediately affects every other. Even in the most primitive areas the bus, the radio and the bulldozer move inexorably in, and when the necessities of world war or world commerce dictate it, anything from the jungles of Papua to the ice fields of the Antarctic can be swiftly taken over and incorporated in the single entity which is the human civilization of today.

What I have said so far touches only the externals of the matter. In truth the process of unification has a more fundamental, more inward character. One can express it by saying that thinking men and women in every part of the world are now aware of belonging to a single history. Negatively, they are aware of standing under the threat of a single disaster which could destroy human civilization as a whole. They are aware that even the smallest border con-flict with one's neighbour is no longer something that one can fight out quietly in a corner; it contains the possibility of escalation into atomic war. Positively (but here one can only speak more vaguely), they share increasingly common expectations about the future, about human rights, dignity, technological development – expectations which they know can only be fulfilled if they are sought for all nations together. Thus positively with some inexactness, but nega-tively with an agonizing sharpness, men see themselves sharing a common history, facing towards a common danger and a common hope. This is something new. There have been, in the past, many attempts to write universal history from particular points of view. There have been men who saw the role of their own nation as the unifier, guide and ruler of mankind. There have been many more who saw history only in terms of the rise and destiny of their own people, the rest of the world being merely background. There have been multitudes for whom history – even if records of some sort were kept – had no real significance at all because human life was understood as an endless cycle in which all things return in the end to their starting-point, thence to set out again on the weary round of meaningless change. And there have been the peoples described by J. L. Myres in his little book, *The Dawn of History*, as 'The Peoples which have no History' – peoples who lived and loved and fought and argued like other men, but who left no records except those that the archaeologist can dig up, because they had no reason to think that anything that happened was worth recording. All of these have existed and do still exist. What is, I believe, wholly new is a situation in which great numbers of ordinary men and women in every part of the world feel themselves to be participants in a common human history, a feeling which does not arise from any belief that their own nation – or any other – is destined to unify the world, but from a feeling that, willy nilly, all men stand under a common danger and all men share (however vaguely) a common hope.

But – and this is the second half of my opening generalization – the fear and the hope are **both** directed towards secular possibilities. Mankind is not being unified on the basis of a common religious faith or even of a common ideology, but on the basis of a shared secular terror and a shared secular hope. One can perhaps most easily introduce a discussion of the positive aspect of this unification – of the shared hope – by looking at the contemporary content of the word 'development'. It is appropriate to do so at this middle point of the United Nations 'Development Decade'. This apparently innocent word deserves more careful scrutiny than it usually receives. The introductory chapter of Zinkin's book *Development for Free Asia* contains an important reminder that before plunging into the detailed questions of economics and sociology which are involved in the development programmes of the Asian countries one should remember that development, in the way in which it is now used, means, for the Asian nations, the deliberate substitution of a new set of goals and values for the traditional ones.[1] One might, in one's sceptical moments, be inclined to question the semantic convention whereby a society which enjoys spending its moonlight evenings dancing in the open air, or listening to songs from the Ramayana, is called an undeveloped society, whereas one which prefers sitting round a television screen listening to songs about detergents is a developed one. But this, of course, is merely trifling with serious matters! For better, for worse, the word development means the pursuit of goals different from those which have been recommended by the main traditions of the non-western world, goals defined in such terms as technical development, industrialization, economic planning, productivity and the more equal distribution of wealth. These are goals which can only be achieved by the sharing of scientific knowledge and by a very large amount of economic planning on a global scale. The pursuit of them draws all races into common involvement in a single universe of thought as well as a single fabric of economic life.

The dynamism of this process is so well known as to require no documentation. It drives merchants, scientists and technical experts of all kinds into every part of the globe. By creating new processes of production it changes the shape of men's lives. By creating new desires it brings unbearable stresses into ancient societies and finally tears them apart. Its effect (not recognized at first) is to destroy the cyclical pattern of human thinking which has been characteristic of many ancient societies and to replace it by a linear pattern, a way of thinking about human life which takes change for granted, which encourages the younger generation to think differently from its parents, which looks for satisfaction in an earthly future. It is in the pursuit of secular, this-worldly goals that mankind is being made one. It is in terms of shared secular hopes and a shared secular peril that we can speak today of the human race as a unity.

Let me illustrate from the experience of India. It will, I

[1] M. Zinkin, *Development for Free Asia*, London: Collins (1958).

think, be helpful to look at the process of secularization
from the point of view of a non-western culture. After
having seen it from that angle, it may be easier to see its
true meaning within western history. When the British began
to build up their commercial empire in India they did their
best to preserve intact the structures of religious belief and
practice which, as they rightly saw, lay at the foundation of
the social life of the country. Hindu and Muslim traditional
law was carefully preserved and administered by British
judges. Every attempt was made to avoid destroying the
pattern by which family and social life were bound in a
single sacral unity around the central core of religious
belief and practice. Temple endowments were protected and
developed, Christian missionaries were, for as long as possible, kept out, and even such inhuman practices as the
burning of widows were protected. But whatever the East
India Company may have hoped, and however profitable it
might be on the short view to their commercial interests to
protect the forms of a sacral society from disruption, they
were themselves agents of a process of secularization which
has proved irreversible. The effect of the exposure of India
over a period of two centuries to the commerce, government, literature, culture and missionary activity of the West
has been to set in motion a process of secularization which
has culminated in the decision of the independent Republic
that India shall be a secular state dedicated to the achievement of a socialist pattern of society.

The statement that India is a secular state means that the
pattern of legislation is no longer determined by the traditional ideas of Hindu or Moslem law. It is determined by
the intention that every citizen, irrespective of his religion or
lack of it, shall be able to participate in the benefits and
responsibilities of a welfare state. Thus legislation has been
passed which is aimed to destroy completely elements in
traditional religious law which are considered incompatible
with this intention, such as untouchability, the dowry system
and so on. These legislative acts, while they certainly lead

public practice rather than following it, express the change which has in fact taken place in the way that Indians think about life. Questions are settled now, not by what is in the Sutras or in the Koran, not by reference to an ultimate religious belief, but by calculations, based on scientific research, of what is likely to be most effective in promoting the dissemination of specific benefits among the greatest number of citizens. A characteristic sentence of Jawaharlal Nehru expresses the spirit which animates this process: 'Whatever ultimate reality may be, and whether we can ever grasp it in whole or in part, there certainly appear to be vast possibilities of increasing human knowledge, even though this may be partly or largely subjective, and of applying this to the advancement and betterment of human living and social organization.' This is the characteristic language of the secular man at his best. It is not a closed dogmatic secularism. It reflects in the thinking of one man who has played an outstanding part in the process, the way in which the ordinary educated Indian increasingly thinks. Whatever one's ultimate beliefs may be (and there is complete freedom to cultivate and express them) one relies on them less and less as a source either of knowledge or of guidance. One concentrates on acquiring the technical knowledge necessary to solve problems one by one as they come along. The question whether one is a Hindu or a Moslem is increasingly unimportant; the main matter is to enlist all the talent available to meet the problems of industrialization, land reform, population control and the rest.

What I have illustrated from the recent history of India is characteristic of what has been happening in most of the non-western world. I do not think that this is the whole picture, as I shall hope to show in a moment, but I think you will recognize it as true as far as it goes. It is what is happening all over what the French call the *Tier Monde*. The outward signs of it are more modern universities, more research institutes, more factories, more governmental and intergovernmental agencies of development. For practical

he may not have wished it quite this way: but this is where we are.

[handwritten top margin: How or where can God be found in this secular history? Perhaps God is using science to do what the Church failed to do — Cyrus]

[handwritten: 17, 18, 19 17 23-5 26, 27 28]

purposes the word 'development' means movement in the direction I have indicated.

By approaching the process of secularization in this way one is perhaps prepared to look at the same process within the western world without some of the emotional tension which the word is otherwise likely to arouse in a Christian gathering. For, of course, in the west the 'sacral society' which has been dissolved by the process of secularization is what we have been accustomed to call 'Christendom'. Here also we have seen the prising loose of one after another of the elements of human thought and action from the direct control of religious principles or of the Christian Church. More and more areas of life have been mapped by the research of those who confessed that they did not need the hypothesis of God for this purpose; more and more of the life of society, of the family, of the individual – including the Christian individual – has been organized without any conscious reference to the Christian faith or the Christian Church. The story is familiar, and so is the reaction of those who see here an insidious enemy against which the Church must fight to recover the lost ground. At the international missionary conference of Jerusalem in 1928, 'Secularism' was put alongside Hinduism, Islam and the rest as one of the rivals with which the Gospel has to deal, but described as the greatest of them. One sometimes reads proposals that the great religions should form some sort of alliance to combat the upstart, a folly which the Jerusalem meeting did not commit though it has been charged with it. But perhaps what I have already said will indicate to you that if one begins by looking at this process of secularization from the angle of a country like India, the problem looks different. The process of secularization in India is accomplishing the kind of changes in patterns of human living for which Christian missionaries fought with such stubborn perseverance a century and a half ago – the abolition of untouchability, of the dowry system, of temple prostitution, the spread of education and medical service, and so on.

[handwritten bottom margin: could secularization be our "Cyrus" — God's messenger?]

[handwritten right margin: Yes; more western world too; (is shall we fight secularization?]

And the same can be said of many other parts of the world.

Missionaries in Asia and Africa have been agents of secularization even if they did not realize it. Like the first Christians who refused obeisance either to the pagan gods or to the divine Emperor, and who were therefore denounced as atheists, their teaching and practice has the effect of disintegrating the sacral bonds that have traditionally held society together. Through their vast educational programmes they introduced into the minds of the younger generation ideas which were bound to call the old religious order into question. At an earlier period the missionary in India would not have put it that way. He would admit, probably, that he intended and expected to replace the pagan society with a Christian one. His mission compounds, his Christian colonies, and his magnificent apparatus of Christian schools, colleges, hospitals and farms were a preliminary sketch for that Indian christendom. He hoped to share with India the privileges of a Christian civilization. But today the missionary in India cannot think that way. His schools and hospitals are dwarfed by those which the State and private agencies have founded. The Christian congregation is no longer content to be identified with a separate colony and insists on being part of the life of the nation sharing with Hindus and others in the task of building the secular welfare state. The ideas of human dignity, of social justice, of the significance of human history, which missionaries brought with them in their teaching of the Bible, have now become the property of those who claim no Christian allegiance, and the effect of these ideas is to discredit and disrupt much that was formally protected by traditional religion. Looking back, the missionary is compelled to recognize that, whether he intended it or not, he has been an agent of secularization. And when he looks at the same process going on within the old Christendom he is compelled to admit that this cannot be treated simply as an enemy to be expelled.

It is significant, therefore, that the recent missionary

conference in Mexico, a lineal successor of the Jerusalem
meeting, which also gave much attention to the question of
secularization, spoke in quite different accents from those
of thirty-five years earlier. It spoke of the process of secularization as 'in its main lines, irreversible' and went on: 'We
are neither optimistic nor pessimistic about this process of
secularization as such. It should not be judged simply by
the criterion of what it does to the Church. Secularization
opens up the possibilities of new freedom and of new
enslavement for men. We have no doubt that it is creating a
world in which it is easy to forget God, to give up all traditional religious practices, and at the same time lose all
sense of meaning and purpose in life. Yet we are over-
whelmingly convinced that it is not the mission of the Church
to look for the dark side and to offer the Gospel as an
antidote to disillusionment. We believe that at this moment
our churches need encouragement to get into the struggle
far more than they need to be primed with warnings. It
simply does not do for us to talk about the problems of
affluence, of too much leisure, and so on, to those whose
backs are breaking under loads we never had to bear.'It is
no longer possible for Christians simply to deplore the
process of secularization; they have to understand it, as the
Mexico meeting tried to do, in the light of the Bible.

Secularization and Biblical History

What is the relation of a secular, this-worldly unification
of mankind to the biblical promise of the summing up of all
things in Christ? Is it a total contradition of it? Is it some
sort of a reflection of it? or perhaps a devil's parody of it?
Or has it nothing to do with it at all?

Perhaps there will be many Christians to whom it would
not occur to pose the question whether the process of
secularization has anything to do with the biblical understanding of the goal of history. The Bible, for them, belongs
to a religious world which is not admitted to belong to the
world of secular events – the world in which we are when

we read the daily newspaper. But this is to read the Bible
wrongly. Whatever else it may be, the Bible is a secular
book dealing with the sort of events which a news editor
accepts for publication in a daily newspaper; it is concerned with secular events, wars, revolutions, enslavements
and liberations, migrants and refugees, famines and epi-
demics and all the rest. It deals with events which happened
and tells a story which can be checked – and is being
checked – by the work of archaeologists and historians. We
miss this because we do not sufficiently treat the Bible as a
whole. When we do this we see at once that the Bible –
whatever be the variety of material which it contains:
poetry, prayers, legislation, genealogy and all the rest – is in
its main design a universal history. It is an interpretation of
human history as a whole, beginning with a saga of creation
and ending with a vision of the gathering together of all the
nations and the consummation of God's purpose for mankind. The Bible is an outline of world history.

For centuries it provided the framework within which
world history was taught in the schools of Europe. Today it
does so no longer. The superficial way of stating the reasons
for that is to say that we now know a thousand times more
about the human story than the biblical writers knew, and
that we have steeped ourselves in the histories of the great
civilizations of Asia whose existence was a mere distant
rumour to them, and that we have far outgrown the narrow
provincialism that thought of Judaea as the centre of the
world. But we must ask a deeper question.

All history is written by selecting out of the almost infinite
mass of recorded or remembered facts that tiny proportion
of them which is believed to be significant for the story.
Even the history of a single city can only be written by
omitting all but a fraction of one per cent of all the recorded
facts from its past and selecting those which are significant
– significant, that is to say, from the point of view of what
the historian believes to be the point of the story, the thing
which gives the city its character, its place in the life of the

nation and the world. A mere sum of all recorded facts is not history.

No one can tell a story well unless he sees the point of the story. The hearer does not see it until the end. How then does one tell the story of the human race when we are still in the middle of it and do not know what the end will be? Can it be otherwise than on the basis of some belief, however provisional, about the point of the story as a whole? And that means a belief which will precisely *not* be a demonstrable certainty. *Only the end denoument can give that*

I confess that I am not impressed by the arguments of those who say that you can get on with telling the story without asking these ultimate questions. Of course you can, but then in fact you are merely failing to scrutinize your own prejudices. I remember spending an evening with a group of teachers in a university in the middle east. It is a university which takes considerable pride in its secular character and its freedom from any kind of religious bias. I was fascinated to discover what were the principles on which they constructed a syllabus of world history there in the country which has been the meeting-point and the cockpit of the peoples of Asia, Africa and Europe, and is now subject to tremendous influence from America, Russia and China. On what principles would one select the materials for a course on world history? What would be the belief about the point of the story which would enable one to select meaningfully from such a vast mass of material? Where would one go for the view of man and his history and his destiny on the basis of which the story could be told? By the time the evening was over I had the impression that if the question was really pressed, the final answer would be *The Readers' Digest*. *What people like to hear i.e.*

If there is to be a true universal history, it will be written on the basis of a faith about the destiny of man which is true. At this point the alternative to faith is not demonstrable certainty but uncriticized prejudice. One can write world history, as H. G. Wells did, in the belief that the

*not faith, they say.
But prejudice..*

*i.e. the Biblical view of history is
Yet a live option.*

on phil. of history.

point of the story is that it finally produces the kind of civilization which H. G. Wells admired. As one can also die, as H. G. Wells did, in utter despair because the point of the story no longer seems worth the travail and suffering of it. The Bible is written in the faith that the point of the story has been revealed in certain events, and that all else that is still to happen and still to be discovered will be truly understood in the light of these events, and that when you have seen the point of the story, all the travail of it is justified.

If, then, the Bible is universal history, what is its relation to the process of secular unification with which we began this chapter? To put the question precisely: is there any relation between the biblical faith about the nature and destiny of man in the light of which it tells the story of mankind, and the beliefs about the nature and destiny of man which are drawing men of all nations today into the sense of participation in a common, universal history?

Let me make three positive points and then put against each of them a question mark.

1) It is a matter of plain record that the beliefs and the techniques which are drawing men together into a single world civilization have their origin in that part of the world which has been most continuously exposed to the influence of the Bible, namely, western Europe. Arab traders have been busy with their commerce in Asia, Africa and Europe for centuries, but it is not Arab commerce which has created the modern international money market. Indian philosophy has a much longer and more distinguished continuous history than anything Europe can boast. But it is not Indian philosophy that has created the modern cosmopolitan university. The Chinese were centuries ahead of Europe in several important technical developments, but it is not Chinese experience and experiment which have created the modern international standards of technology. It is a plain matter of fact that the peoples of any country in the world today can participate in the process of what is called development only by learning a European language and

mastering techniques of study, experiment and research
which have been developed by the European peoples.

There is no reason to think that the races of western
Europe, so recently and so imperfectly elevated from a state
of barbarism, have any innate superiority in these matters.
Other races, notably the Japanese, have shown that they
can in a few decades not merely equal but surpass the European in many of the skills which are characteristic of modern
world civilization. I am speaking here not merely of the
technical skills which make Japan today the world leader
in certain branches of electronics and instrument manu-
facture, but also of the matters where the language barrier
makes it more difficult for the rest of the world to follow
Japanese advances in thought. There is no reason to attri-
bute the leadership of western Europe in the development
of the modern world civilization to any special endowment
of skill or intelligence. But there is good reason to believe
that the rise of modern science and technology was directly
related to the beliefs about the created world and about
man's place in it which are distinctive of the Bible. It could
not occur in Europe until the grip of the Aristotelian world-
view upon the European mind had been broken. It is
difficult to believe that it could have occurred at all within
the world-views of the dominant Asian religions.

The German physicist C. F. von Weizsäcker, in discussing
the issues involved in the famous trial of Galileo, writes as
follows:

Scientists of those times liked to invoke Plato against
Aristotle in defence of their belief in mathematical laws. . . .
To Plato only pure mathematics has any claim to be called
true cognition, the real claim being reserved for the philo-
sophical theory of the forms; of the sense world nothing
more than a likely story can be told. To Galileo mathematical law holds strictly in nature and it can be discovered
by an effort of the human mind which includes the perform-
ing of experiments. Nature, being complicated, does not
always offer us the simple cases in which the one law we

want to study is free from disturbances. But these disturbances, being caused by forces that obey their own laws, are equally open to mathematical study. Go on dissecting nature and you will be its master. The realism of modern science is neither a naïve belief in the senses nor is it an aloof spiritual disdain of them.

There is a theological background to this attitude. The world of the senses is the world of nature in the Christian sense of the word. Platonism and Christianity both rely on what is beyond nature. But there is the difference that Plato's God has not made matter; only the spiritual element in the world is divine; hence science, being a divine gift, does not apply to the material world in a strict sense. To Christians God has made everything. Hence man, made in his image, can understand all created things, that is, certainly the whole material world. The very idea that the Word has been made flesh, the dogma of Incarnation, shows that the material world is not too low to be accepted by God and hence to be understood by the light of reason given us by God.

Later he writes:

. . . The concept of exact mathematical laws of nature which was only dimly present in Greek thought gained far greater convincing power by means of the Christian concept of creation. Thus I think it is a gift of Christianity to the modern mind. Now we see how this inherited gift is used against the religion whence it came. And this killing of one's own parent by the weapon inherited from him becomes more and more naïve. Kepler was a sincere Christian who adored God in the mathematical order of the world. Galileo, and even more Newton, being a more religious man, were sincere Christians who were interested in God's work. But while Galileo had still to defend his right to read God's greatness in the book of nature, Newton had to defend his idea of nature as a book written by God. Modern scientists in general find it very difficult to think of a religious interpretation of natural law as anything but an additional tenet, probably mythical and certainly not logically connected with the concept of laws of nature. No good will and no religious fervour can reverse this development. Modern secularized reality can in fact be interpreted in terms that take no account of religion at all. Science does not prove the existence of God. This should never be forgotten by those who want to understand the modern world in religious terms. On the other hand it will be good to see that the tree on which this now floating seed of modern science has grown was Christianity; that it was a sort of Christian radicalism which transformed nature from the house of gods into the realm of law.[1]

It is surely unfortunate that so small a place is given in our schools and colleges to the study of the origins of modern science. If the western world took more seriously the duty of trying to understand the origins of the science which so dramatically shapes the whole of our lives, there would be some hope that the peoples of Asia and Africa would also become interested in the subject. At the present time we witness everywhere the following paradoxical situation. Non-western peoples are eager to master every element in the science and techniques of the western world, but are almost totally uninterested in enquiring into the roots of the tree on which these fruits have grown. Western man, apparently embarrassed about his ancestry like a schoolboy who is embarrassed about his parents, goes out of his way in his contacts with the rest of the world to avoid any suggestion of commitment to the religion of the Bible, but shows himself passionately interested in studying the minutest details of the origins of the non-western religions and cultures. Yet his study of them is always with the tools of thought which western science has developed and not with the tools of the non-western cultures and languages. We are accustomed to listen, for example, to an anthropologist who has specialized in the sexual practices of some primitive community rebuking the provincialism of the Christian moralist who imagines that the biblical norms of conduct are the norms for the whole of mankind. But he

[1] C. F. von Weizsäcker, *The Relevance of Science*, London: Collins (1964), pp. 106-7, 120-1.

So 1. Science due to Biblical world view. It's only requiring history that gives *** think we can have the plant without its roots. — Thus God – Yahwih is related to scientific culture.

26   *Honest Religion for Secular Man*

would not thank you if you took him too seriously, and proposed that he should likewise drop the principles and methods of anthropology as he learned them in the London School of Economics and use instead the anthropological concepts of the Samoans or the Papuans. It is to be hoped that a time will come when, both in the west and elsewhere, it will be recognized that the study of the origins of modern science is of at least as much importance to an educated man as the study of Caesar's wars or Vergil's poetry. When that time comes there will be less need to argue the relation of the Bible to the roots of the scientific world-view.

2. The second positive affirmation which I wish to make is as follows. An essential ingredient in the process of secularization is the dissemination of the belief that the conditions of human life can be radically bettered. In one form or another the idea of the new order just beyond the horizon is what gives power to the movement of development. I have already drawn attention to the fact that this innocent-sounding word 'development' really covers, for the non-western peoples, a far-reaching shift of allegiance. It means that standards of judgment are radically changed. Things which had been venerated for centuries are discarded, and things which were once considered fit only for the interest of menials are the subject of concern for statesmen. The study of theology, of philosophy, of classical poetry and music, is neglected, and great new institutions are created to train men in scientific agriculture, sanitation and metallurgy. If one stands back to look at this in the perspective of the centuries, it is an astounding thing that such ancient civilizations as those of India, China and Japan, which have for thousands of years withstood the shocks of invasion and defeat and yet retained their identity, should in the space of a few decades undergo this radical overturning of their traditional hierarchies of value. We are witnessing before our eyes the dissolution of forms of human society which had seemed for centuries and even millennia to be as solid and unchangeable as the earth itself.

And if one asks where is the source of the thrust that could achieve this astonishing result, there is no doubt about the answer: it is the faith that it is possible to create a new order of human existence in which poverty, disease and illiteracy are banished and all men can enjoy the privileges of what are called the developed nations.

This faith is not a product of any of the ancient religions of Asia or Africa. These have not, in the main lines of their teaching, encouraged their adherents to expect a radical change in the conditions of human existence. There are, it is true, important strands of thought within the complex web of Hinduism which encourage serious concern with the affairs of this world, and modern Indian writers are properly eager to draw out the significance of these for the facing of today's tasks. But it cannot be denied that the main thrust of the teaching of the ancient Asian religions has been away from a concern to change the world. Their dominant teaching has been that the wise man is he who seeks to be content with the world, to be released from attachment to it, but not to seek to change it. The idea of total welfare for all men as a goal to be pursued within history is foreign to the Asian religions, and modern Indian writers such as Sarma and Panikkar have no hesitation in acknowledging that, so far as India is concerned, it is part of the western invasion of the last few centuries. It is a secularized form of the biblical idea of the Kingdom of God. It is rooted in that understanding of human history as the sphere of God's redeeming acts which sets the Bible apart from all the other sacred literature of mankind.

3. For my third positive statement I turn to the remarkable book of the Dutch scholar, A. T. van Leeuwen, entitled *Christianity in World History*.[1] The thesis of this work, which covers an astonishing range of history and anthropology, is that the process of secularization is the present form in which the non-western world is meeting biblical history. His interpretation of biblical history is centred in

[1] London: Edinburgh House Press (1964).

natural history sees what is as ordained by
God. Scientist sees it not so -- but has the idea
of Kingdom of God · Yst as model for change

28   *Honest Religion for Secular Man*

the struggle of the prophetic faith in the living God to
overcome what he calls the ontocratic pattern of society. By
this useful phrase he designates the pattern of society which
rests upon a total identification of the orders of society with
the order of the cosmos. All the great human civilizations
which have developed from the neolithic period onward,
except in so far as they have come under the influence of
the prophetic critique, have rested more or less upon this
identification. Outwardly this pattern is typified by the
Babylonian Ziggurat and its analogues in other ancient cultures, which is at the same time the navel of the earth, the
seat of government and the centre of the cult, and by the
virtual identification of priest and king. Van Leeuwen illus-
trates the ontocratic pattern in a wide-ranging survey of
the ancient civilizations of China, India, Mesopotamia and
Egypt, and shows how the Hebrew kingdom also took over
the main features of the ontocratic pattern. But he shows
how the central theme of the Bible is the prophetic attack
upon this pattern in the name of the living God whose rule
can in no way be identified with any earthly rule, and
whose will is not completely embodied in any human pattern
of society. He traces the same struggle down through the
history of the Christian Church, and shows how, especially
in the Byzantine form of the Christian civilization, the ontocratic pattern reasserted itself in a Christian form, but how
– especially in the stormy history of the western Church –
that pattern was always broken open again by the living
power of the prophetic tradition, nourished in the Bible.
And within this framework of ideas he sees the present
worldwide process of secularization as a decisive movement
in the age-long struggle of which the Bible records the
critical centre. Now for the first time these ontocratic
societies of Asia which had endured with little break for four
or five millennia are being disrupted and opened up to
influences which challenge their very existence. It is a
moment as decisive for human history as the neolithic
revolution which laid the foundation for these great civiliza-

tions. Something irreversible is happening. The ontocratic society is doomed. Mankind will no more accept the identification of the powers of the cosmos with the powers of any socio-political order. The triumph of secularization is certainly not the triumph of the Kingdom of God; but neither is it simply the work of the devil. It is, says van Leeuwen, the present form in which the non-western world (hitherto firmly held within the ontocratic pattern) is meeting the impact of that attack upon the ontocratic pattern whose centre and source is to be found in the biblical story. Men have given up the pretension of primeval religion that they could build a tower with its top in heaven. It is, says van Leeuwen,

> a reductive move without parallel, and one which gives to the activity of building a city and a tower – dispossessed now of its ultimate religious purpose and meaning – a kind of obsessive intensity springing from the conviction that man is engaged here in an impracticable enterprise, unfinishing and unfinishable – but which for that very reason is forever exacting the toll of an impossible, unfinishing and unfinishable effort on his part. That is the glory and the desperation, the greatness and the wretchedness too, of the technocracy which has ousted ontocracy. The spell of a divine universe is broken; upon every temple falls the devastating judgment that it has been 'made by man'. Even modern science has to do simply with a man-made universe. It moves among the stars and probes the inmost secrets of the atom; and in all this man comes face to face with himself.

Let me remind you that the question which we are at the moment trying to answer is the following: Is there any relation between the biblical faith about the nature and destiny of man in the light of which it tells the story of mankind, and the beliefs about the nature and destiny of man which are drawing men of all nations today into the sense of participation in a common universal history? I have made three positive statements:

(1) That there is strong historical evidence to suggest that

the roots of modern science and technology are in the biblical understanding of man and nature.

(2) That the driving power of the movement which is drawing all men into the single world civilization is a secularized form of the biblical eschatology. *Marxism too*

(3) That the dissolution of the 'ontocratic' pattern of society in the non-western world can be understood as a new phase in the history of the fight of prophetic religion against the total claims of a sacral society, that is, a society completely unified around a religion and a cosmology.

But these affirmations prompt a series of questions which I want now to try to formulate.

Three Questions

(i) I want to put first a question concerning the relation of modern science and technology to the biblical understanding of man and nature.

I shall never forget a conversation with a man who was a member of the team of physicists in Chicago who worked on the first atomic bomb during the final years of the last world war. He described to me what it felt like to work on the job with his colleagues, and the mounting excitement as success came nearer. And then he described the sudden change of feeling which came over the whole team when they realized that they had succeeded, and that the thing they had created was potentially the most monstrous evil that the mind of man had ever conceived and brought forth. The nature of their work imposed absolute secrecy. They were precluded from sharing their sense of guilt and anxiety with anyone outside. They were all physicists and had never given to questions of ethics the sort of sustained and precise study that could have satisfied their own exacting standards as scientists. He told me how they formed a series of groups to study every aspect of their problem, historical, ethical, religious, legal; how they bought and devoured treatises on subjects they had never studied before; how they finally wrote to President Truman urging that the bombs should be used on some uninhabited area after due warning and not in any case on a city; how their letter was never even answered; and how they had to see the instrument they had created used to create the horrors of Hiroshima and Nagasaki. They found that at the moment of their apparent triumph they were simply tools for an operation against which their moral sense revolted.

The memory of that conversation has always been with me as I have tried to reflect on the place of science and technology in our world. That sudden swing from an exultant sense of mastery to an appalled feeling of guilt and anxiety is surely typical of much more than this particular incident. A good deal is written at present about man's coming of age. Much of the traditional language of biblical religion is written off as belonging to a period when man felt himself unequal to the task of mastering his environment and when he had perforce to invoke the aid of alleged supernatural powers. Today, by contrast, it is suggested that man has grown out of this childish mentality. Today he knows how to control the powers of his environment. He does not pray to be delivered from disease or from drought; he gets himself inoculated or he builds irrigation works.

But this is only half the truth. To see the whole truth of the situation you must read the fiction of our time, as well as the scientific and technical journals. You must attend the theatre as well as the seminar. You must consult the psychiatrists as well as the cyberneticians. When you do this it is clear that there is another side to the picture. Alongside of, or perhaps underneath, the sense of mastery, the assurance that we are only at the beginning of the developments made possible by modern techniques, there is also a sense of something like meaninglessness and even terror as man faces his future. This at least seems to me to be true of the most developed societies. One does not need to be a cynic to notice that the suicide rate varies from nation to nation in something like a direct ratio to what is called development. Suicide is on the one hand an assertion of mastery

[handwritten marginalia: Man is still man— guilt— fear it.]

[handwritten marginalia: If man is, in fact, the new god, we're in real trouble. Wally-pursue this. Show how deny-ing man is... Conclude—but it's still good word.]

[handwritten note at bottom: Sermon! next Sunday.]

because it denies that man is finally responsible for his life to another; and on the other hand it is a confession that the burden of this mastery is too heavy to be borne, because without responsibility there is no meaning, and if there is no Other, there is no responsibility.

The roots of modern science lie in a society shaped by the biblical understanding of man's place in the natural world. The New Testament has its own account of man's coming of age. 'During our minority,' says St Paul, 'we were slaves to the elemental spirits of the universe, but when the term was completed, God sent his own son, born of a woman, born under the law, to purchase freedom for the subjects of the law, in order that we might attain the status of sons' (Gal. 4.3-5). The possibility that man might be the master of the created world is not contemplated; the two possibilities are slavery and sonship.

The adult status which, according to Paul, is offered to men in Christ is on the one hand a deliverance from bondage to elemental powers. On the other hand it is an invitation to responsible sonship of the Father in whose hands all created things, all so-called powers and forces, and all history lie. It is therefore an invitation to deal boldly and confidently with the created world and all its powers. It is a deliverance from pagan fear of the mysterious powers of the cosmos. It is a desacralizing of the natural world which sets a man free to investigate, and experiment and to control. There are no more gods, demi-gods or demons presiding over the various aspects of the natural world. All belongs to God, serves his will, is plastic in his hands. And man is invited, if he will, to become God's son and heir and to have the freedom of the whole estate subject only to his obedience to the Father.

It is not surprising, therefore, that the missionary in Asia and Africa has been at the same time the pioneer of technical development. It was in the shelter of the mission compounds of the nineteenth and early twentieth centuries that new crops were introduced, new techniques of cultivation developed, and new industrial skills taught. The freedom to make revolutionary changes of this kind came along with liberation from bondage to the sacral powers presiding over the natural world. Perhaps it is difficult for one who has known no other world than that of western Europe to realize what that liberation means. Nothing is more striking in the testimony of new converts from pagan cultures than this sense of liberation from the power of the dark forces which rule over the natural world, this new freedom to serve one master who is both just and good, whose will is not an inscrutable and unintelligible caprice, but a purpose of good which can be believed and in growing measure understood. And this desacralizing of nature is the precondition for the development of a vigorous science and technology.

In the Bible this desacralizing is attributed to what God has done in Jesus Christ. According to St Paul, God has, in Christ, dethroned the cosmic powers and liberated man from their control so that he can enjoy, through Christ, the freedom and responsibility of sonship. This way of speaking has no meaning at all for the majority of those who now exercise the freedom of dealing with a desacralized nature by the methods of modern science and technology. The desacralizing process lies buried so deep in the history of modern civilization that the ghosts of the old powers no longer trouble them. The natural world is to be dealt with in itself and without reference to any supernatural entities. And there are Christians who urge us to accept this state of affairs without question. The process of secularization, they say, must be carried right through to the end. The religious ideas and images of the Bible, even the idea of a God who is other than man and sovereign over man, must be given up. The Christian, too, must deal with the world *etsi Deus non daretur*, as if there was no God. The process of secularization will not stop short with the dissolution of the pagan religions; it must dissolve what Christians have understood by religion itself. Man has come of age and has *[handwritten margin note at top:] 1. Has man really come of age? Is there not evidence that he needs a living God — to whom he feels responsible — who has given freedom; permission to control nature the way — !*

[handwritten note:] has technology really driven God out .. or only showing us how much we need him

no need of the idea of God to help him deal with his environment.

Against this I want simply at this stage to put one question. Are we taking seriously into account the other side of the picture, the sense of meaninglessness and even of terror with which modern secularized man faces his future? Was my Chicago friend not typical of the best of modern man in his combination of rejoicing in the skills that could produce a controlled nuclear reaction, and his foreboding at the sense that he and his colleagues were releasing a demon which was more likely to destroy mankind than to be the servant of mankind? Is it wholly an accident that, precisely in the most highly secularized and scientifically advanced countries, the practice of astrology has a great contemporary renaissance? And is it not a significant part of the total evidence, that while medical science has succeeded in mastering all but a few of the organic and functional diseases, psycho-somatic and mental diseases are outstripping the curative resources of medicine, and that this advance of mental disease seems to be in direct proportion to the advance of modern technological development? Is it quite certain that the ancient possibility has been finally excluded, namely, that man might be the slave and not the master of the powers of nature? Is it quite certain that the ancient gods are buried beyond the possibility of haunting us again?

(ii) My second question is posed with reference to the affirmation that the driving power of the movement that is drawing all the nations into a single history is a secularized form of the biblical eschatology, a belief in some sort of new order towards which history is moving.

This affirmation seems to me to be unquestionably true as regards the developing countries of Asia and Africa. They are spurred on to make the radical and often painful and costly changes in their ways of life demanded by their programmes of development by the faith that thereby a new order will be made possible, an order radically different from all that they have known before. But, with the experience of Europe before us, one is bound to ask how it will be possible for these nations to escape the dilemma that seems to be built into the idea of a new order within history. The dilemma is a familiar one and it can be stated simply. If the supreme good in relation to which all things are valued is a state of society yet to be realized, how can one avoid the devaluation of the actual human person as he now is, and the resulting destruction of his freedom? Will a society which takes this goal of development seriously not find itself ineluctably driven towards some sort of ideology as the only means of evoking the necessary sacrifices, and will not every such ideology involve eventually a process of dehumanization?

One of the noblest examples of the secular spirit at its best is Jawaharlal Nehru. It is due to him more than to any other man that the Indian Republic has been able to move in the direction of a genuinely secular state, and that India is among the few nations recently emancipated from colonial rule which still manifests a genuinely democratic public life in which the different political parties offer the electorate a real freedom of choice between different national goals. While he was at the helm he was able to resist the pull of ideological passion both from the right and from the left and to maintain a truly secular spirit in Indian politics. But this record stands out as an exception in the political evolution of the new nations, and Nehru was himself the product of an almost entirely western and Christian education. One is compelled to ask: Will even India be able to escape the pull of some ideology either of the right or of the left? Will it be possible to evoke from that nation of four hundred and sixty millions the unity and the self-denial that will be required if the agreed national goals are to be achieved without the pressure of a powerful ideology? The experience of the developing nations makes it difficult to give an affirmative answer. The pressure is all the time in the direction of some sort of messianism, either of the

2. *If the new order becomes the supreme good in itself — what is to protect it; the people in it from becoming demonic — for all men into slavery to it. If God is over it — a higher court of appeal — it cannot de ueturate.*

cf 36   *Cl. Birch*

Honest Religion for Secular Man

nation, of the leaders, or of the communist revolution. The genuinely secular spirit can be sustained in a society where the supernatural motives for mutual service which the biblical revelation evokes are widely operative; it has yet to be shown that it can sustain itself against the pressures of ideology in a society which is seeking, as the new nations are, to achieve rapid advance towards the conditions of a welfare state.

(iii) My third question concerns the rapid dissolution in the non-western world of what van Leeuwen calls the onto-cratic pattern of society. The contact of the West with the non-western world has brought with it not simply a new pattern of society which might replace the traditional one, but rather a new revolutionary principle which questions all settled social structures. It has provided not only the weapons with which Hindu reformers like Ram Mohan Roy could attack the evils of Hindu society in the early nine-teenth century, but also the weapons which Gandhi used against the British Raj, and the weapons with which the younger generation in India today attacks the rule of the Congress party. The same prophetic spirit which refuses to accept injustice because it is entrenched behind the authority of the state is invoked in each case. What has come into India – to take only this example – is not simply a new pattern of society, but a question directed against every pattern of society; a permanent principle of revolution. There can never be again anything like a sacred order binding the whole life of society in a quasi-religious unity unless it is the result of some post-Christian totalitarian ideology.

our country exactly.

The question which I want to pose in regard to this is the following: where is the positive ground upon which it is possible to sustain this perpetual question directed against all actual forms of society? Men must live together some-how or other in societies and nations. And such societies must necessarily protect themselves from attack. Man cannot live by negation alone any more than he can know by doubt alone. The positive basis of the prophets' critique of society

Good

use xxx

in their day was the word of the living God: 'Thus says the Lord'. Only from that affirmation could they proceed to negation. Only because God is higher and greater than any human society, and only because God *is*, could the prophet speak about negation, and announce even the total destruction of the society to which he belonged.

I believe that van Leeuwen is right in seeing in this prophetic attack upon the ontocratic pattern of society the element in the Bible which makes biblical faith a secularizing agent. In other words, I think there is a real continuity between the prophetic resistance to the claims of a sacral kingship, the Christian refusal to acknowledge the divinity of the Emperor, and the secular spirit which refuses to acknowledge the final authority of any sacred tradition or any official ideology which overrides the right and the dignity of the human person. My question is whether the truly secular spirit can be sustained if it loses contact with that which gave the prophet his authority to speak — namely a reality transcending every human tradition and every earthly society, a God who is for man against all the 'powers'.

It is difficult to make this point because in the moment of making a protest or a denial we are apt to be unconscious of the affirmations which are tacitly assumed. There is a close parallel here with the place of doubt in scientific enquiry, and since this is also an important element in the secular spirit it is worth spending a little time on it. If we examine the functioning of our own minds when we are in the act of doubting a belief which we have hitherto taken for granted, we shall find that we can only doubt its validity if, for the moment, there are other beliefs which we do not doubt. If we could for a moment doubt all our beliefs together we should be reduced to imbecility. A rock climber makes progress by letting go a handhold or a foothold one at a time while he searches for a new grip. While he does so his whole attention is on the hand or foot which is groping for a new hold, but in fact he depends upon the other three holds to which for the moment he is paying no heed. If he were to try to let go of them all together he would be lost. Just so the processes of doubting and re-thinking by which we advance in understanding depend upon beliefs which for the moment we do not doubt but simply take for granted.

Something similar holds good for the process of moral protest against things as they are. The negation will become self-destructive if it does not rest upon an affirmation which is, for the moment, not questioned. The inexhaustible power of the prophetic spirit in the tradition of biblical faith was derived from a tremendous affirmation – namely the affirmation of the reality and power and holiness of God who is other than, greater than and more enduring than any human institution or achievement. My question is: if that affirmation be denied, can the secular spirit end otherwise than in a self-destructive nihilism?

In putting these three questions, which are really different aspects of one question, I am in effect declaring my belief about the meaning of the worldwide process by which mankind is being at the same time unified and secularized. I accept in its main outlines the thesis of van Leeuwen that this process has a real continuity with the biblical-prophetic history. In so far as it rests upon the freedom of man to exercise a delegated authority over the natural world without fear of any 'powers' other than the Creator himself; in so far as it seeks the freedom, dignity and welfare of man as man and challenges all authorities which deny this common human dignity; in so far as it brings all mankind into a growingly interdependent unity of life; this movement of worldwide secularization is a genuine continuation of that liberation-history which is the central theme of the Bible. Just for that reason I am driven also to believe that this movement is misunderstood if it is seen out of that context; that it will recoil in self-destruction. Specifically I suggest (Question 1) that if the mastery which is given to man through the process of secularization is not held within the context of man's responsibility to God, the result will be a new slavery; (Question 2) that if the dynamism of 'development', the drive to a new kind of human society, is not informed by the biblical faith concerning the nature of the Kingdom of God it will end in totalitarianism: and (Question 3) that if the secular critique of all established orders is not informed and directed by the knowledge of God it will end in a self-destructive nihilism.

The idea that the new freedom which secularization brings might be destroyed by a renewal of the ancient pagan bondage of man to sub-human powers may seem somewhat mythological. But it corresponds to realities in our present situation. It is not, for example, accidental that in the 'developed' nations there is a great revival of belief in astrology. Astrology offers an answer to questions which men are bound to ask, and for which science can in principle give no answer. Even if it were possible to conceive, like Laplace, of a mind that could know the movement of every particle in the universe and could describe the entire chain of causality lying behind every event that ever happened in the universe; even – in other words – supposing one could 'explain' everything that ever happened, there would remain always an unanswered question. That is the question which the human person cannot help asking: why was it to me, to my child, to my home that this happened? The 'explanation' which science can provide has no place in it for an answer to that question. There is no place for the word 'I' in a text-book of physics. One is sometimes told that this is a question which ought not to be asked because there is no answer to it. That is merely to confess the bankruptcy of thought. Questions about personal destiny, about the meaning and purpose of human life, will always be asked, whatever the umpires of the language game may say. If there is no doctrine of divine providence then the vacuum will be filled by some kind of belief in luck, in fate, or in the stars.

The Polish Marxist philosopher, Adam Schaff, complains that Marxists in his country have been unable to answer the *reply to positivism breaks upon the rock of the human question.*

questions raised by existentialism because they have tried to deny that the problems exist. This, says, Schaff, is like trying to deny the existence of America. It is merely a confession that your rules of thought have broken down. Speaking of the questions which ordinary people are compelled to ask, he says:

> It is possible to shrug this off with a compassionate smile as nonsense. And yet the words echo a problem which simply cannot be ignored. Nor can the questions 'Why?', 'What for?', which force their way to the lips of people tired of the adversities and delusions of life. This applies still more to the compulsive questions which come from reflection upon death – why all this effort to stay alive if we are going to die anyway? It is difficult to avoid the feeling that death is senseless – avoidable, accidental death especially. . . . From the point of view of the progression of nature death is entirely sensible. But from the point of view of a given individual death is senseless and places in doubt everything he does. . . . Attempts to ridicule all this do not help.[1]

Belief in astrology comes in to fill this vacuum. The ancient pagan world into which the Christian Gospel first came saw human life in terms of the conflict between virtue and fortune. On the one side was the implacable and ultimately irresistible power of the world external to man, into which man is thrown without his willing or deciding it. On the other side was the courage and skill and wit that a man could bring to the ultimately hopeless conflict. It was the triumph of early Christian thought, expressed in the doctrine of the Triune God, to replace this picture by a quite different one. This did not, like some of its competitors, offer an escape out of the world by a purely religious route. It offered an interpretation of human life in terms of which the centre was the revelation of God's Word in Jesus Christ. What man had to deal with was not an impersonal fate, but the One whose mind and purpose had been made manifest

[1] Adam Schaff, *A Philosophy of Man*, London: Lawrence and Wishart (1963), p. 34.

in Jesus. And this same mind and purpose could be given to man through the Spirit to work as an inner principle guiding and sustaining him. Man's life was no longer governed by fate, or the stars, or any other power. It could be lived wholly within the revealed mind and purpose of the Triune God. If that possibility is destroyed, it is inevitable that some form of the ancient pagan belief in fate should come in again to answer the questions which cannot be silenced as long as man remains human.

In the present chapter I have tried to indicate grounds for thinking that the process of secularization is rightly understood in the light of the biblical understanding of the human story, and that – following the statement quoted from the Mexico Conference – we are to recognize in it both new possibilities of freedom for man, and also new possibilities of enslavement. This means, therefore, that the Christian must view the process of secularization neither with fear and hostility nor with uncritical enthusiasm, but with a sober understanding founded upon his biblical faith. I do not, in the present discussion, propose to study the view of those Christians who see this whole process of secularization as a defeat for the Christian faith. I can sympathize with, but cannot share, this view of the matter. No one but a fool would close his eyes to the injury to human persons and the loss of precious elements in the human heritage which mark the process of secularization. These are part of the human situation with which the Church in its pastoral responsibility for men must try to deal. But I do not believe that it is in accordance with the biblical faith to try simply to resist or reverse the process. Nostalgia for what is disappearing is understandable. But neither the metaphysical systems with which the confession of the Christian faith has been associated in recent centuries, nor the social and political structures which we have inherited from the period when Christianity was the established religion of Western Europe, belongs to the essence of the faith as we have to confess it today. Believing in the God who is the Lord of history we ought to have every confidence in seeking rather to understand, in the light of his revelation of himself in Jesus Christ, what this process of secularization means, and to find the ways by which, in this new situation, we can bear witness to his purpose.

However, this cannot mean that we simply accept the process of secularization as though it provided in itself the norms by which belief and conduct were to be determined. We cannot accept the position that the ultimate norms for our thinking are provided by 'what modern men and women can believe'. Our starting-point is God's revelation of himself in Jesus Christ as this is testified in the Bible. We have to reinterpret the biblical texts so that they enable us to understand what the eternal Lord is saying to us now – to us who no longer belong to a world dominated by religious belief. In the next chapter I want to engage in discussion with some who are endeavouring to do this. I shall maintain that while the effort in which they are engaged is a necessary effort, it is in danger of being fruitless because of a failure to interpret correctly the meaning of the process of secularization and its relation to the biblical revelation. I shall try to indicate my concern by examining three closely interrelated points.

1. In the Bible God speaks to man as one who belongs to the texture of human history as a whole. God's call to him is to take his part in fulfilling God's purpose for mankind, not simply to find authentic existence for himself. Current attempts to restate the Gospel for secular man, influenced by existentialism, emphasize rather the situation of the individual in his aloneness.

2. In the Bible God addresses man through 'mighty acts' – events of history in which God's will and power are made manifest to faith, and which become the foundation on which faith rests. Current attempts to restate the Gospel in secular terms find the idea of 'acts of God' unacceptable.

3. In the Bible God speaks to man as one who is Another – man's vis-à-vis who addresses him and calls for his re-

sponse. Current attempts to restate the Gospel in secular terms attempt to translate this biblical language into terms which eliminate the idea of 'another' who is 'out there'. ✗

I shall argue that this is to misunderstand the nature of the process of secularization and to offer to the Church precisely the wrong guidance for its present tasks.

2

A CRITIQUE OF CHRISTIAN
RESPONSES TO SECULARIZATION

The New Individualism

THE Bible speaks of God's calling of the individual in the
context of his purpose for all the nations. No one can doubt
that the Bible takes seriously the individual and his responsibility for decision. No existentialist could complain
that the solitary responsibility of each man to give his
answer to God is not fully acknowledged. But if one thinks
of the great moments of the Bible where an individual is
confronted with the calling of God, the question at issue is
never just his own destiny; it is God's purpose for his people
and through them for mankind. Abraham's call is to be the
founder of the nation through which all the nations will
bless themselves. Moses is called to be the liberator of an
enslaved people. The great prophets are all called to be
God's messengers to the people and politicians of their time.
The apostles are called by Jesus to be his messengers to the
nations. The calling of the individual is not simply for the
acceptance of his own personal destiny; it is for the fulfilment of his role in God's plan for the salvation of mankind.
It is a calling to responsible participation in the events
which are the key to world history.
But the most influential attempts to restate the Christian
Gospel in terms supposed to be intelligible to modern
secularized man have proceeded by using the concepts of
existentialist philosophy. The whole emphasis is upon the
spiritual situation of the individual and the Gospel is pre-
sented as the means by which the individual in his loneli-
ness can find the freedom for responsible living. The whole

attention is centred not upon the public history of mankind, to which, according to the Christian faith, the biblical history, the history of Israel, of Jesus and of his apostles, is the key; but rather upon the personal spiritual history of each believer. Listen, for example, to a characteristic passage from Professor Bultmann:

> We possess the present through encounter, and encounter implies the necessity of decision. . . . We are confronted with the eschaton in the Now of encounter which is neither an eternal nor a timeless present nor a nearer or remoter future. Here indeed is the paradox of the faith of the New Testament. . . . Eschatology tells us the meaning and goal of the time process, but that answer does not consist in a philosophy of history, like pantheism, where the meaning and goal of history are to be seen in each successive moment, or like the belief in progress, where the goal is realized in a future Utopia, or myth, which offers us an elaborate picture of the end of the world. Indeed eschatology is not at all concerned with the meaning and goal of secular history, for secular history belongs to the old aeon, and therefore can have neither meaning nor goal. It is concerned rather with the meaning and goal of the history of the individual and of the eschatological community. Moreover the meaning is fulfilled and the goal is attained in the *fullness of time* — that is wherever the word of the proclamation establishes an encounter.[1]

At this point I confess that I am tempted to ask whether Marxist thinking would not provide more useful concepts for a restatement of the Christian message to a secularized world than do those of existentialism. The latter are characteristic of the present political and spiritual situation of the western world. They make little appeal in the developing countries which are filled with hope about what is possible within history. They emphatically do not provide the weapons that Christians living under Marxist régimes can

[1] Rudolf Bultmann, *Kerugma and Myth*, London: SPCK (1962), p. 116.

[handwritten margin notes top: Existentialism removes / all hope. / It capitulates to despair. It is a fatal compromise -- for it surrenders the gospel -- the very thing it hoped to make palatable to modern man. a capitulation to pagan philosophy.]

use to fight their ceaseless battle. But they express perfectly that loss of conviction about any real meaning in human history which is characteristic of the so-called 'free world', and which explains – I believe – much of the sense of futility which weighs upon the affluent societies of the West.

For that sense of futility there are intelligible reasons. We have witnessed the collapse of the doctrine of progress. We have revolted from the absurdities and immoralities of the totalitarian systems which are the residuary legatees of nineteenth-century liberalism. We are without conviction about any worthwhile end to which the travail of history might lead. Into such a vacuum, the existentialism which offers to the individual some hope of meaning for his personal life has an easy entry. But I submit that it is a mistaken policy that thinks to find an entry for the Gospel into the mind of secularized man by flying the colours of existentialism. The Gospel is vastly more than an offer to men who care to accept it of a meaning for their personal lives. It is the declaration of God's cosmic purpose by which the whole public history of mankind is sustained and overruled, and by which all men without exception will be judged. It is the invitation to be fellow workers with God in the fulfilment of that purpose through the atoning work of Christ and through the witness of the Holy Spirit. It calls men to commitment to a worldwide mission more daring and more far-reaching than that of Marxism. And it has – what Marxism lacks – a faith regarding the final consummation of God's purpose in the power of which it is possible to find meaning for world history which does not make personal history meaningless, and meaning for personal history which does not make world history meaningless. Only an interpretation of the Gospel which puts in the centre God's total purpose for human history is true to the Bible, and I am persuaded that only such an interpretation can meet the realities of a world in process of secularization – and I speak of a whole world, not merely that affluent fraction to which we belong, but equally the peoples struggling to achieve development

[handwritten margin notes left: So the existential gospel, purporting to make faith easier, betrays the true gospel.]

[handwritten note bottom: Existentialist individualism (me only) my happiness + occult mystaecism = ends in no social passion.]

Good material to use on the treatment
God of history

and the peoples – more than a third of the whole – whose
whole lives are shaped by the philosophy of Marxism.

The Escape from History

The Bible speaks of acts of God in history. It is, in its
main outline, a continuous record of such acts. In the Old
Testament the central act is the deliverance of Israel from
slavery to the tyranny of Egypt at the crossing of the Red
Sea; in the New Testament the central act is the raising of
Jesus from the dead. But these are the climactic acts in a
story in which God's mighty power is seen at work throughout the whole history of the chosen people.

This way of speaking has always been totally unacceptable to the main tradition of pagan philosophy. Stories told
to illustrate timeless truths about the nature of the world
and the duty of man have always been acceptable. But the
idea of a God who somehow reaches out his hand to inter-
vene here or there in the affairs of the world has been held
by the majority of philosophers to be an impossible an-
thropomorphism. The famous word of Pascal, found sewed
up in his jacket after his death, tersely expresses the contrast
I am making: 'Fire! Not the god of the philosophers! The
God of Abraham, the God of Isaac, the God of Jacob.' No
one who reads the Bible as a whole with any attention can
doubt that this is the fire which burns at its heart: the
belief in a God who acts and who is therefore related in a
special way to certain names and certain events. And no one
can read what is being written in our time to interpret the
Gospel to modern secularized man without noting that at
this point the writers are generally on the side of the philosophers rather than of Pascal. Let me quote again from
Bultmann:

> The saving efficacy of the cross is not derived from the fact
> that it is the cross of Christ; it is the cross of Christ because
> it has this saving efficacy. . . . How do we come to believe
> in the saving efficacy of the cross? There is only one answer.
> This is the way in which the cross is proclaimed. It is always

proclaimed together with the resurrection. Christ meets us in
the preaching as one crucified and risen. He meets us in the
word of preaching, and nowhere else. The faith of Easter is
just this – faith in the word of preaching. It would be wrong
at this point to raise again the problem of how this preaching
arose historically, as though that could vindicate its truth.
This would be to tie our faith in the word of God to the
results of historical research. The word of preaching confronts us as the word of God. It is not for us to question its
credentials. . . . In accepting the word of preaching as the
word of God, and the death and resurrection of Jesus as the
eschatological event, we are given an opportunity of understanding ourselves. . . . The real Easter faith is faith in the
word of preaching which brings illumination. The resurrection is not in itself an event of past history. All that historical
criticism can establish is the fact that the first disciples came
to believe in the resurrection. . . . But the historical problem
is scarcely relevant to the Christian belief in the resurrection.[1]

Here the Christian faith is set forth as a body of beliefs
which stands by itself apart from the question whether or
not certain events actually happened. The only important
thing is that the 'Easter faith' authenticates itself as true in

---

[1] Rudolf Bultmann, op. cit., pp. 41-2. I realize that it is difficult
for those who read and write in English to do justice to thoughts
originally expressed in German, in which there is a distinction
between the *historisch* and the *geschichtlich*. The English translator
of Ebeling's book, *Word and Faith*, expresses the distinction thus :
'*Geschichtlich* means belonging to the succession of events, while
historisch means accessible to or connected with, the methods of
scientific historical research.' Dr Alan Richardson, and other English
writers, have questioned the propriety of this distinction, holding
that the implied 'methods of historical research' are in fact false
methods resting upon a positivist interpretation of history which
historians themselves reject. Richardson argues very convincingly
(*History, Sacred and Profane*) that German Protestant theology has
got itself into an impossible position through accepting a false theory
of the nature of historical study. Commenting on the fact that the
English language has only one word to do duty for the German ones,
he says : 'At least the English usage helps to remind us that there is
only one history and to prevent us from thinking of an abstract
history, in which facts have no existential significance, alongside a
suprahistorical sphere which lies outside the scope of historical
scholarship' (op. cit., p. 155).

the mind of the hearer, because it illuminates for him his own situation. It does not matter whether or not the first disciples were deceived in thinking that Jesus had risen from the dead. The event is the *belief* of the first disciples, not the object of that belief. The belief is equally authentic, even if it was belief in something which did not happen, in fact even if it was false. Faith concerns the individual in his self-understanding; it does not stand or fall with what happens in the history of the world.

I submit that this is precisely the *wrong* way to re-state the Christian message for modern secular man. I submit that the protest of Pascal is as valid against those who dissolve the Christian message into an existentialist philosophy as against the philosophers whom Pascal had in mind. This particular kind of existentialism is a post-Christian phenomenon, but the attempt to rest on ultimate beliefs which are untouched by the events of history is characteristic of ancient paganism. In contrast to all such timeless philosophies, ancient or modern, I submit that the restless dynamism which has created and sustains the worldwide movement of secularization is fed from the biblical faith in a meaningful history, ultimately in a God who acts in history and who therefore gives history its meaning. In the Bible faith is not self-understanding. It is commitment to serve God in the events of secular history. It is response to his call to specific obedience in fulfilling his purpose for mankind. It is faith in the God who acts in history, and whose acts are the clue to its meaning and direction.

I may be permitted to illustrate what I have to say on this point with a personal reference. I think it is impossible to live for long in India without becoming conscious of the tremendous power of the kind of spirituality which has its roots in the *Vedanta*, the spirituality which seeks the eternal by means of escape from that which changes and decays, which seeks the motionless centre from which one can watch without involvement the ceaseless and, strictly speaking, endless movement of the circumference. No one who has felt the power of that reverent spirituality will treat lightly the possibility which Christopher Dawson suggested many years ago that the whole of western civilization, if it lost its living relationship with the biblical faith, could be re-absorbed into the monistic spirituality of Asia. The fact that this seems much less likely now than it did when Dawson wrote more than thirty-five years ago, is an illustration of the truth in van Leeuwen's thesis that the world-wide extension of the process of secularization, which has proceeded with such immensely accelerated speed in the past twenty-five years, is a form of the impact upon the non-western world of the biblical history. But in support of Dawson I would say, on the one hand, that there is ample evidence to show that the constant and reiterated reading and preaching of the Bible breaks down in the minds of ordinary Hindus the cyclical, non-historic, way of thinking and replaces it by a way of thinking which is dominated by the idea of God's acts in fulfilment of his purpose – in other words, by a linear way of thinking about the world of change; and on the other hand, that it is quite common to find in India men trained to the highest level of knowledge and competence in western science and technology who yet retain as the basic and determinative form of their thinking the cyclical, non-historic pattern of advaitist Hinduism.

There are two main lines along which the mind of man can seek a resolution of the tension which he experiences between the evanescent and the eternal. He can interpret the eternal as a motionless centre equidistant from every point on the moving circumference; or he can interpret it as personal will which moves towards the fulfilment where all that is now opposed to it will be wholly subdued to it. Each of these interpretations corresponds to something in man's own experience. We can withdraw from the jangling multiplicity of events and experiences into an inner quiet where we experience only the unity of undisturbed consciousness. To seek the perfection of that experience has been the goal of the dominant tradition of Indian spirituality. Or we can throw ourselves into the events of this changing and decaying world in the belief that out of this something can be fashioned which answers to our own vision of what is true and right. The former course requires no revelation in history to sustain it; the very idea of such a revelation is incompatible with its quest for the extinction of all duality in a single undifferentiated consciousness. But the latter becomes mere barren self-assertion if it is not rooted in some assurance that my purpose is not just my purpose imposed upon the stuff of things, but is my response to the purpose for which all things exist. And to speak of purpose is to speak of a personal will known by words and acts which express and foreshadow the achievement of the purpose, words and acts which express and foreshadow something which is not yet visible but which is real now and will be visible at the end. It is to speak, in other words, of revelation. This is the way the Bible speaks. And my contention is that the dynamism of the worldwide movement of secularization is rooted in the biblical faith which understands human history in terms of the mighty acts of God for the fulfilment of his purpose; and that, by the same token, to offer to men in the midst of a secularized world a version of the Christian faith denatured by the removal of the idea of the acts of God is to misunderstand completely both the Christian faith and the movement of secularization. It is the characteristic offer of a civilization which has lost its sense of direction and its belief in the future.

But what, exactly, do we mean if we talk of 'God's acts in history'? We do not mean, certainly, a series of events which are separable from the whole fabric of human history, a *Heilsgeschichte* which is separate from the history of the world. No such separation can be made, for the whole fabric is woven as one piece. The events described in the Old Testament are, from one point of view, simply part of the material which the archaeologists, the cultural anthropologist, and the historian of the middle east take as the data for their study. The crucifixion of Jesus is, from one point of view, simply one of the thousands of executions carried out during the Roman rule in Palestine. In what sense do we speak of these events and others as acts of God?

The only possible answer, I think, is that we speak of acts of God because in this or this situation we are made aware in an exceptional way of the working of the personal will which is at work in all things, and that we *believe*. This answer is, of course, not an explanation or a definition; it is simply a testimony, a confession. At this point, as at all points of ultimate decision, nothing else is possible. There is no possibility of demonstrating that in such and such event God was at work. Indeed, unbelief is always a much more likely possibility. Almost the whole of the Old Testament from the Exodus onwards is the story of the unbelief of Israel. The children of Israel are depicted as being sceptics about the reality of God's activity almost from the moment that they got safely across the Red Sea. The almost uniformly disastrous story of Israel during the centuries which followed might seem to be a confirmation of this scepticism, and the whole struggle of the prophets whose teaching has given us the main substance of the Old Testament as we have it, was to restate and reinterpret for each new situation the basic Exodus faith that God was indeed at work in the history of his people for the sake of the whole world. It was a faith maintained against what might seem overwhelming facts to the contrary, brought to its most daring universalism precisely at the moment when the Israelites were homeless slaves living under the shadow of the Babylonian empire.

This faith did not seek escape from the appalling present realities of slaughter, exile and slavery by flight to a timeless religion independent of the events of secular history; it announced the impending victory of God within and over all the events of history by which both politics and nature would become manifestations of his just and merciful rule. It did not simply look within for inner peace; it looked upwards and forwards for its vindication in the victory of God.

Finally, One came who announced that victory was at hand. And we are familiar with the sequel. He was rejected by Israel, betrayed and deserted by his disciples, charged both as a blasphemer against God and a rebel against the Emperor, and executed as a common criminal. There, one could well imagine, would be the end of this faith in a God who acts in history. But in fact it is that event which has become the central point of attention for those who interpret history in terms of the acts of God. And it is so because Jesus rose from the dead.

For our present argument the resurrection of Jesus is the crucial issue. For the traditional understanding of the Christian faith, this is the mighty act of God *par excellence*, the one on which faith completely depends. For many who are seeking to reinterpret the Christian faith in terms acceptable to a secularized society the resurrection is the stumbling-block which has to be eliminated. I want to argue that this betrays a profound misunderstanding of the real issues which the process of secularization presents to the Christian faith.

Men who have been dead and buried for three days do not rise again from the dead and behave as the risen Jesus is alleged to have behaved. This fact was well known before the rise of the modern scientific world view. It is really rather absurd to suggest, as Bultmann does, that a man who uses electric light cannot believe things like this. It is no more and no less difficult to believe in the resurrection after the invention of electric light than before. Nor is this belief made more or less credible by the abandonment of the belief that the universe has three storeys and the world is flat. All of this talk is irrelevant to the issue. It has never at any time been possible to fit the resurrection of Jesus into any world view except a world view of which it is the basis. This does not answer all the questions, but it eliminates a certain amount of nonsense. The resurrection is an event which you only really believe if every world view based on any other starting-point has collapsed. It was so for the first apostles, and it has never been otherwise for any generation since.

One believes the resurrection on the basis of the historical evidence, which is the testimony of the first disciples and of the early Church. This evidence is much stronger than that which we have for much of what we accept as history. If we reject it, we do so because, on other than historical grounds, we believe that the resurrection cannot have happened. It is sometimes said that the resurrection is an event outside history. This seems to me simply a sentence without any meaning. If it happened it is not outside history. It is also said that an irrefutable demonstration, for instance, of the fact that the tomb was empty would not be the same as the faith of the apostles in the resurrection. This is true; but it is also true that an irrefutable demonstration that the body of Jesus was decaying in the tomb, or somewhere else in Jerusalem, would have sufficed to kill the Gospel message on the spot, and would have precluded the coming into existence of the Christian faith in any sense in which we have known it.

Professor van Buren in his book *The Secular Meaning of the Gospel* seeks to reinterpret Christianity in such a way that Christians can participate in the secular civilization of our time without the encumbrance of religious beliefs which he finds impossible. He does not believe that Jesus rose from the dead, but believes that—even while the body of Jesus was decomposing—the scattered and disillusioned disciples somehow discovered on their own a fresh experience of the contagious power of Jesus which created the Christian Church. This is, of course, a very old attempt to explain the existence of the Church without belief in the resurrection. Any person is entitled to hold this opinion, but it ought not to be recounted as though it were history. It abandons the only historical evidence available in favour of an imaginative reconstruction of what Professor van Buren,

[handwritten margin note:] Yes — it forsakes what history we have on the subject & turns to fancy.

on the basis of his present beliefs, thinks must have happened. The Christian tradition is based on the evidence of witnesses about what happened, and stands or falls with it. Like many others before him, Professor van Buren's Jesus is an imaginative creation, not a figure who ever actually lived, and those who do not share the Professor's beliefs will find the figure unconvincing.

But can one really believe that Jesus rose from the dead? No—not if your starting-point is somewhere else. But if, like the first apostles, you have come to a point where every other foundation has been knocked away, and you have no coherent understanding of experience in which you can live and act with hope, then you may find that the testimony of the apostles is not only credible, but in fact the only rock on which you can begin to build. Perhaps, for example, you have come to the point where you are helplessly impaled on the dilemma of action within history to which I referred early. On the one hand, how can one secure determined and effective action to achieve a new order of society within history without invoking the power of an ideology which dehumanizes man and treats him as a means rather than an end? On the other hand, how can you treat seriously the personal destiny of every human being without robbing human history as a whole of any intelligible meaning? How can you have meaning for history as a whole except by surrendering the meaning of each human life, or how can you have meaning for each human life except at the cost of meaninglessness for human history? If you have felt that dilemma—which for me is always felt most acutely when I go back and forth through the notorious Berlin Wall and contrast the grim totalitarianism on the one side with the screaming futilitarianism on the other—then you will perhaps understand that you might be driven to belief in the resurrection as the only possible foundation for a faith which takes seriously both the destiny of mankind and the destiny of every human soul.

The resurrection of Jesus is our assurance that belief in

God is not simply an affair of the soul withdrawn from the public life of mankind. It is the ultimate security for a belief in the reality and goodness of the created world. St Paul says it is the assurance that our labour is not, in the end, futile. Faith in the resurrection is, in this sense, the guarantee of the validity of the fruitfulness of the labour of science and technology to understand and master the natural world for the service of mankind. For it is not fanciful to suggest, as Christopher Dawson did, that the loss of this faith that God acts in history could in the long run destroy the dynamic of modern western civilization and leave it to sink back again into the timeless monism of the ancient pagan religions of Asia. Many western thinkers, wearied by the intolerable burden of a meaningless affluence, would not have to travel far in order to come to anchorage in that ancient harbour where there are tides but no currents, where there is consciousness of change, but no conviction that the change can bring mankind nearer to any worthwhile goal.

The Denial of the Other

Throughout the Bible God remains always other than man, confronting him with a will not his own, addressing him and calling for response, commanding, rebuking, forgiving, comforting, judging and saving. God loves and cares for man, and men are created to love and honour God, and this is possible because God is other than man, because he is not a part of man or a creation of man's hands or of man's mind, but in truth man's vis-à-vis, the one who speaks to man and whose word alone gives man his being and his humanity. God is there, *out there* if you like, even though he is closer than breathing and nearer than hands and feet. Turn which way he will, man is confronted by God who is not himself but another.

Once more it is characteristic of current attempts to restate the Christian faith in terms of intelligible to men in a secularized world that they play down this element in the biblical picture. The Bishop of Woolwich has announced that our image of God must go, and has explained that he means the thought of God who is 'out there'. He takes the true statement that God is the ground of our being as an invitation to abandon the way of thinking of God which sees him as 'there' and to think of him as 'here' – in the depth of our own consciousness.

Professor van Buren considers that the word 'God' should only be used, if at all, in inverted commas. His understanding of Christian language about God is that it expresses a non-cognitive *blik*. The word blik happens to be the Dutch word for a view, but in this case we are to use the word only when nothing is seen. Believers must, says van Buren, be careful to make clear what they mean by the word 'God'. 'If "God" is not a word which refers to something, they should be careful not to use it in a way that suggests that it does. If they are talking about a "blik" rather than about "how things are" they should say so.'[1] These sentences make it clear that the qualifier 'non-cognitive' is important. The Christian blik does not give a vision of how things are. It implies that intention to act in a certain way. It does not enable the Christian to make statements about 'how things are'.

It is important to recognize the truth which these writers are concerned to assert. The word 'God', as Christians use it, does not 'refer to' an object, an entity about which we could make statements comparable to those which we make about the world known to us through our senses. Christian language about God is not of the same kind as language about things which are the objects of our experience or reflection. This means that Christian language about God is different from the vast majority of human language about 'God' and 'the gods'. For the great majority of the human race in the past, and even in the present, 'gods' are entities about which one can speak in the same way as one speaks about other

---

[1] *The Secular Meaning of the Gospel*, New York: Macmillan; London: SCM Press (1963), p. 106.

great personages of whom one has heard. For most of the biblical writers the existence of these beings was a matter of course, as it is for vast numbers of people today who have not yet been radically secularized. Modern secularized man, however, is unable to believe in the existence of these beings. From the point of view of faith in God as it is confessed in the Bible, this change is part of the outworking of that revelation of the living God in whose light these so-called 'gods' are seen to be non-entities. The matter is not otherwise if we go on to speak of the various forms of theism which have existed and do exist even in our secularized world. The word 'God' has stood for one element in a total system of thought in such a way that statements could be made about the nature of this being, and his relationships to other beings, within a total system of ontology. While, from the point of view of a student of comparative religion, Christianity may be classified as a form of theism; from the point of view of the Bible this god of theism may be as much a human construct as the idols of the nations. Just as it has become impossible for modern secularized man to believe in the existence of the gods of the polytheist pantheon, so it is becoming impossible, or at least abnormal, for him to share the view which until recently was normal in western society that there exists some sort of supreme being controlling the affairs of the world, about whom one can make objective statements comparable to those which one makes about mathematics or physics. The fading away of this belief is no more disastrous from the point of view of biblical faith than is the fading of the belief in the 'gods'.

We are therefore completely in agreement with the writers whom we are criticizing that belief in God is not a matter of statements about the existence of an object beyond the reach of science. Belief in God is a matter of confessing that one has been known, loved, called, redeemed by Another whom one only knows because he has so acted. Christian statements about God are not comparable with the statements we make about objects in the world of things or of ideas, statements, that is to say, about objects which we can grasp, manipulate, and even attempt to control. They are statements which confess what he has done, which invite others to confess him and to worship him. They are statements arising out of a context of personal engagement to another. The only analogies available to us here are those drawn from the realm of personal relationships. To use these analogies is not to relapse into a lower form of speech than the language of abstract thought. Because we are human beings, all human language is anthropomorphic, and it is wholly arbitrary to suggest that the language of personal relationships is more anthropomorphic than that of abstract thought. They are both anthropomorphic: the relevant question is, which is more appropriate for the matter in hand? For the purpose of speaking about God, the appropriate language is that of personal relationships.

The language in which a lover addresses his beloved, or speaks about her, is not the language of scientific observation. On other occasions the doctor, the psychiatrist and the tailor may have to describe the same person, but the language will be different. The lover's language cannot be checked simply by referring to the tested observations of these others. His language describes, if you like, a *blik*, a way of looking at her. It tells you about him as well as about her. But he will be rightly indignant if you tell him that it is a 'non-cognitive blik', that his language is in fact merely a statement about his own emotions, sentiments and intentions, but that it says nothing about anything outside himself. He will not be able to *prove* the contrary; he can only continue to protest against an interpretation which destroys the whole meaning of what he is saying.

The Christian is in much the same difficulty with regard to the so-called atheist interpretation of the New Testament. If it is said that his statements about God are not statements about an object, he will agree. But if it is further said or implied that they are in truth only statements about his own *blik*, or about the ground of his own being; if it is said that there is really nothing and no one *there*, then he can only protest that this is to destroy completely what it is supposed to interpret. As Gollwitzer[1] has pointed out, this atheistic interpretation of Christianity is as irrefutable as the denial of the reality of the outside world by a solipsist epistemology. The Christian can only insist that his language means what it says, that there is another who loves him and whom he loves, who redeemed him and to whom he is responsible.

It will be clear that what we are talking about is not the god of general theism, but the God who is revealed in the great saving deeds to which the Bible testifies, the God whose face has been unveiled for us in Jesus Christ and whose love has been manifested in his dying for us on the Cross. It is this personal, living, saving God who has made his name known to us, about whom we are speaking. If the word 'God' really refers only to some aspect of human experience, to something which is discoverable by reflection upon the general human situation – even if that something be defined as our ultimate 'concern' – then it is difficult to see why we should quarrel about whether the word 'God' is used or not. In that case the dispute is simply a semantic one. The question of belief in God is no longer a matter of conversion : it is simply a matter of definition. Against this the Christian believer can only reply that the God of whom he speaks has more serious issues to raise.

I therefore find myself in agreement with Harvey Cox in his stimulating book on *The Secular City* where, in a passage in which he criticizes van Buren, he writes :

> The summons to accountability before God . . . precludes . . . the verbal byplay in which theologians sometimes try to convince contemporary nontheists that the differ-

---

[1] Helmut Gollwitzer : *The Existence of God as Confessed by Faith*, Philadelphia : Westminster Press; London : SCM Press (1965), p. 102. The whole argument is the best treatment of this subject that I have read.

ences among men today over the reality of God are merely verbal. They are not. Although to the neutral observer there may appear to be no difference between the God who absents himself, who refuses to bark at man's whistle, and the no-god-at-all; there is all the difference in the world. Given the fact that man in dialogue fashions the meanings by which history proceeds, that he is free to take responsibility for history, one utterly crucial question remains: is this responsibility something which man himself has conjured, or is it *given* to him?

The biblical answer of course is that it is given to him. For the Bible, after mythological and metaphysical overlay has been scraped away, God is not simply a different way of talking about man. God is not man, and man can only be really *'response*-able' when he *responds*. One must be responsible *for* something *before* someone. Man, in order to be free and responsible, which means to be *man*, must answer to that which is not man.[1]

I agree with Cox in insisting, as against van Buren, that the question between theists and nontheists is a question of substance and not simply a question of language. It is the question whether I am in the last resort accountable to another who is not myself—not even the depths of my being—and whether this accountability is not in fact what constitutes the humanity of man. It is indeed possible to deal with the material world, and with human persons, as though such accountability to another did not exist. Modern scientific thinking is generally dominated by the ideal of a kind of knowledge in which personal commitment and responsibility would play no part. In this climate Christians have found it hard to defend the biblical picture of man and his world, which is utterly dominated by the universal presence and power of the One to whom man is responsible, who created all things, who calls man into his service and by whose word man is made truly man; but who is likewise the One whose voice is in the thunder, whose handiwork is spread out nightly in the heavens, whose chariot is in the

[1] Harvey Cox, *The Secular City*, New York: Macmillan; London: SCM Press (1965), p. 259.

storm; the One, in short, with whom man has to do in every phase of his being, whether in his most intimate personal relationships or in his dealing with the world of politics or the world of nature.

The Christian concern to insist upon the reality of God in the biblical sense is at the centre of the struggle for the integrity of man as man. A view of the world from which this has been eliminated can have no final safeguard for the human person. In a technologically advanced society what is to prevent the planners from treating human beings as significant only from the point of view of the plan? If, as we are often told today, thinking has to be functional rather than ontological, what stands between us and a society in which human beings are treated simply according to their usefulness to society? During World War II, Hitler sent men to the famous Bethel Hospital to inform Pastor Bodelschwingh, its director, that the State could no longer afford to maintain hundreds of epileptics who were useless to society and only constituted a drain on scarce resources, and that orders had been issued to have them destroyed. Bodelschwingh confronted them in his room at the entrance to the Hospital and fought a spiritual battle which eventually sent them away without having done what they were sent to do. He had no other weapon for that battle than the simple affirmation that these were men and women made in the image of God and that to destroy them was to commit a sin against God which would surely be punished. What other argument could he have used? What are we to say of that most characteristic feature of the 'developed' societies – concentration on the young and contempt of the old? It is a logical outcome of a purely functional view of man. It is difficult to see what are the grounds upon which a consistent secularist would refuse to take the final logical step and approve the painless elimination of those who have ceased to perform a significant social function.

The concern to insist upon the centrality of the personal, the refusal to surrender the 'supernaturalism' of the biblical picture of God as the living and sovereign Other who is the source of all being, is a concern for the real humanity of man. Perhaps Protestant Christians in recent years have, however, been at fault in trying to defend this concern on a too narrow front. From the Jewish philosopher Martin Buber we learned the phrase 'I and Thou', and learned to see something of the depth of a personal relation and of the distinction between the knowledge which we can have of another person and our knowledge of the world of things. In face of the overwhelming pretensions of science to give a complete picture of the world from which the possibility of a personal God has been eliminated, it was natural to draw attention to the reality of the world of personal relationships as a world in which knowledge did not follow the prevailing pattern. It is perhaps now becoming clear that, as is true in respect of other areas of thought, the retreat into a position thought to be safe from attack has been a mistake. Our knowledge of persons cannot be isolated from the wholeness of our knowledge of, and dealing with, the world. What is now clear is that it is not merely our knowledge of persons but our whole knowledge of a reality beyond ourselves which rests upon commitment to and accountability to an Other, and that if this be denied, man's humanity itself is in the end denied.

Cox, whose book is built upon a three-stage theory of human history – tribal, urban, and 'technopolitan' – sees the phrase 'I and Thou' as characteristic of his middle, or urban, phase. Tribal man was in a 'pre I-Thou' condition. 'The deficient individuation of tribal man prevents his experiencing God as fully "other".'[1] In the second stage of human development, 'God is seen as one who has authority *over* me. The relationship is one of confrontation.' Now, says Cox, we are in a new stage characterized by a new type of interpersonal relation. This occurs in the 'work-team' which is typical of modern technological culture, the team of people pooling their skills to solve a particular problem.

[1] Op. cit., p. 263.

This new human situation will, says Cox, affect our sym-
bolization of God. We must think now of an 'I-you' relationship, in which God is willing to be our partner, our fellow
team member in doing what needs to be done in the world.

I confess that I find Cox's three-stage version of human
development unconvincing, and suspect that this final product of it was necessitated rather by loyalty to the scheme
than by insight into the human situation. It is indeed true
that the kind of working team of experts which isolates a
particular problem and works together for a limited, temporary solution is characteristic of a secular and technically
developed society. But Cox is building too much upon this
fact. Three comments are in order:

1. The factors which enable a team to work together as
a coherent whole include loyalties which go beyond the
team itself. To be an effective member of such a team, a
man must acknowledge a responsibility to the truth as he
sees it, to right as he understands it, even when this may
involve clashes which could break up the team.

2. Relationships within such a team go beyond purely
functional relationships. They must include compassion,
forgiveness, loyalty. In spite of Cox's justifiable suspicion
of the attempt to introduce 'the family spirit' into an
organizational team, it remains true that a team will break
down if it knows nothing of these elements which make life
in a family possible.

3. Over the 'technopolitan' society whose liberties Cox
celebrates there hovers the formidable possibility of the
enslavement of man. Totalitarian states also employ the
technique of the expert team for limited purposes. God is
not just a member of the team. He is the One to whom
each member of the team is responsible, to whom an answer
has in the end to be given. He is the 'Thou', or – better – the
'I', who can never be an object of planning, can never
become an 'it', the One with whom in the end every man has
to deal.

The prophetic, biblical understanding of the human situation is nowhere more vividly expressed than in our Lord's parable of the Sheep and the Goats. What we are told there is that behind the most insignificant human being stands the living Lord himself, to whom we have to render final account. The technopolitan society will end in disaster if it does not recognize the reality which is set forth in that parable. To say that is not in any way to underestimate the enormous possibilities for new human freedom and dignity which are opened up by modern techniques of social planning. It is simply to say that these new techniques make it more necessary to insist upon the truth of the biblical picture of the human situation – namely that at every point in his life man is confronted by and is accountable to One who is not himself, but who is his maker and Lord.

To see the world in this way is, if you like the word, a *blik*. It is not to claim the existence of an object beyond the reach of the telescope and the microscope, but rather to claim that the telescope and the microscope cannot give an exhaustive account of the reality with which we have to deal; just as when I feel that for the first time I have come to know another person as a real person, I am not claiming to have discovered an additional object beyond what could be detected by the surgeon or the psychiatrist. There is no reason whatever to quarrel with the assertion that we are here dealing with a *blik* which involves the intention to act in a certain way. Where I have to differ from van Buren is in his repeated statement that this *blik* is non-cognitive. On the contrary, I believe that this biblical way of looking at things gives true knowledge of things as they are and as we have to reckon with them.

Christian statements about God are, according to van Buren, announcements of an intention to act in a certain way which arise from contemplation of the events recorded in the Gospels. When a Christian speaks, therefore, about love to God, he is simply adopting a particular way of speaking about love to his neighbour. The two commandments, love to God and love to neighbour, are two ways of saying one thing. In commenting on Bornkamm's statement that to equate the two commandments in this way is to turn the word God into a mere symbol, van Buren remarks: 'This is closing the barn door several centuries too late.'[1] Precisely. The word God is a symbol which we might so well dispense with. Instead of talking about loving God we should simply talk about loving our neighbours and stop there. What has in the past been called love to God has no other meaning.

This way of speaking of belief in God is rather widespread among those who seek to restate the Gospel for a secular age. The season for it is understandable. Nothing is more revolting than the spectacle of pious professions combined with conduct which denies them. The Bible is full of prophetic denunciations of precisely this combination of official piety and practical godlessness – what Isaiah calls 'iniquity and the solemn meeting', or, as you might say, 'sin and Sunday observance'. And St John says bluntly: 'If a man says I love God and hates his brother, he is a liar.' But there is an essential distinction between this prophetic attack on false religion and what van Buren is saying. The prophets speak as they do because God IS – because there is a personal will which is not my will but which has authority over my will, a will which I can disobey (and do disobey) but which I *ought* to obey. Van Buren does not believe this, but tries to keep his relationship to the Christian faith by saying that these prophetic words are really a mythological way of announcing the intention of the speakers to act in the way indicated.

I must simply say that this seems to me to be untrue. One may disbelieve these prophetic words 'Thus saith the Lord' and deny that there is anyone involved except the prophet himself. But one cannot blandly alter them to 'The following is my programme' and pretend that the meaning has not been changed. The change of meaning is in fact a momentous one. Let me put it in this way.

[1] Op. cit., p. 183.

I believe that God's will for me is that I should behave in the way which is a response to what he has done in Jesus Christ, and I believe that this is his will for all men. Because of this I know that I *ought so* to behave, and therefore in my best moments I do *intend* so to behave, though the intention is never perfect and is sometimes totally perverse. In fact I do not so behave. I constantly disobey what I know to be the will of God. Because it is a matter not merely of my intention, but of God's will, the will expressed in Jesus Christ, there is room and need for the whole relationship of repentance, forgiveness, and asking for fresh strength, so that even my perversities become the way by which I am cleansed of self-love and enabled with a more consistent intention to love my neighbour.

But if in truth there were nothing in this business but my own intention, I do not see what ground I would have for taking it so seriously. In the first place my intentions are extremely mixed, weak and changeable. In the second place, there are other people in the world with other intentions. There are, or there have been, those for instance who intend to liquidate the Jews and maintain inviolate the colour bar. If there is nothing in this matter except my intention, why should I seek to resist them and assert the propriety of my intention over against theirs, any more than I insist upon my preference for coffee without sugar and my dislike of Coca Cola?

An often quoted passage in one of Bertrand Russell's earlier writings runs as follows:

> All moral rules must be tested by examining whether they tend to realize ends that we desire. I say ends that we desire, not ends that we *ought* to desire. What we 'ought' to desire is merely what someone else wishes us to desire – parents, schoolmasters, policemen and judges.[1]

Lord Russell did not share with van Buren the disadvan-

---

[1] Bertrand Russell, *What I Believe*, London: Kegan Paul (1925), pp. 37f.

tage of being a professor of theology. He was not obliged
to show that his statements were really just a modernized
version of the language of the Bible. It is even doubtful
whether he really meant what these words say. His life has
been an impressive denial of them. But he shares with van
Buren the denial of the central Christian belief in God, the
belief, therefore, that there is involved in our moral decisions more than our own intentions or desires, more than
the pressures of the desires of nursemaids, schoolmasters
and policemen; that in our moral decisions we have to do
with a supernatural will which is not ours but that of our
Creator. If we insist upon this, insist, that is to say, that the
biblical language about God cannot be simply translated
into statements about my intentions, we must first agree
that it is nevertheless true that the nursemaids, schoolmasters and policemen are very much involved in our moral
decisions. We begin by taking our moral judgments from
our parents and teachers. But we start to learn, at a fairly
early age, to distinguish between pressures upon us which
represent merely what someone else wants, and pressures
which represent what ought to be. Only by so learning to
distinguish do we become morally responsible persons able
eventually to resist overwhelming pressures to conform to
the standards of society and eventually, if need be, to lay
down life itself for the sake of that which is believed to be
right. It is through men that everyman has to learn to know
the will of God, but the true fruit of that knowledge is to
know that he must obey God rather than men. When he
knows that he can live a truly mature life of freedom and
responsibility.

If I am labouring this point it is because it is vital for a
true understanding of, and response to, the process of secularization. Secularization is a process in which men are set
free from total envelopment in sacral forms of society—
forms, that is to say, in which it is believed that the form
of society fully represents and mediates the purpose of God
for human life. Secularization sets men free to question, to

experiment and to make independent decisions. It requires of the individual man a capacity to take decisions which, in traditional sacral societies, he would not have to take. It is a summons to greater personal freedom, and to the responsibility which freedom entails. *Jn 1 "darkness cannot overcome it*

Here I am again frankly accepting van Leeuwen's biblical interpretation of the process of secularization. I am viewing it as the present form of the attack upon the ontocratic form of society which is the central theme of the Bible. I am seeing it in terms of the Johannine portrayal of the coming of Jesus as the coming into history of the light by which all men are finally and personally exposed and judged. From this point of view I am compelled to regard van Buren's programme for a secular reinterpretation of the Gospel as completely misconceived. It rests on a failure to understand the process of secularization in its biblical perspective, and its restatement of Christian belief would, if accepted, destroy the possibility of a creative Christian participation in the process of secularization.

For in a secular society much more depends upon the personal responsibility of the individual than in a sacral society. There is no single pattern of belief or conduct to which he is compelled to conform. It is a plural society in which not only different religious beliefs but widely different moral standards co-exist. And therefore the question becomes the more urgent: what is the authority for my choices? Is there anything more in them than simply my own intention? If not, can the fabric of society be held together? Will it not be simply torn apart by the pull of contending programmes? Of course, the old sacral structure which has endured for centuries is not going to disappear over night. It provides a capital which it will take some time to dissipate. The pull of traditional beliefs and moral standards will not immediately cease, even in the most radical process of secularization, and in time of stress it will be exploited even by those who are engaged in destroying it. But eventually the question will have to be faced:

what is the authority for the decisions which individuals are required to make?

As a Christian I answer that the authority is the will and nature of God revealed in Jesus Christ. The authority does not lie in my will, but in a will which is not mine, which I ought to obey, which I frequently do not obey, and which can nevertheless forgive. To state that all of this language is really a mythological or pre-scientific way of describing my intentions, and that the real facts can be exhaustively described by saying: 'I intend to behave in the following way', is a mere assertion which will not bear examination. Let me illustrate this at three points.

1.) If my decisions can appeal to no authority beyond my own intention, it is difficult to see why I should resist the intentions of others when the cost to myself is likely to be excessive. There is, in fact, nothing to prevent the secular society from being taken over by some sort of ideology which enforces conformity by sheer pressure. Arthur Koestler in his book *Darkness at Noon*[1] has vividly described what happens when the conviction is destroyed that any authority for decisions exists beyond the will of the strongest power. Martyrdom is, in its proper meaning, witness to the existence of an authority which, though hidden, has right of way even over life itself. If there be no recognition of such an authority, nothing can prevent the secular state from becoming the demonic caricature of a sacral society – namely a society ruled by a post-Christian totalitarian ideology.

2.) If there is in reality nothing in the Christian's affirmations about God except the affirmation of an intention to act in a certain way, then there is no place for the forgiveness of one's opponent. The true mark of Christian action in the world, that which saves it from pharisaism and fanaticism, is that it combines the recognition that God requires me to act, with the recognition that I am a sinner who constantly misinterprets or disobeys God's will and so re-

[1] London: Jonathan Cape (1940).

quires constant forgiveness. This means, therefore, that, while resolute in action, I must at the same time forgive the man who acts against me. In other words, my knowledge of God contains in it something which goes beyond the conviction that I must act in a certain way; it requires of me a certain kind of acceptance of the man who absolutely opposes my way of action.

This becomes a very real issue in situations like the one which is now being faced by Churches in the United States. It is very painful to Christians to have to acknowledge that the same areas of the United States in which racial segregation is at its worst are also the areas in which a certain kind of evangelical piety has its strongest hold – in which there have been and are great revival movements, great conversions, and great manifestations of personal piety, which have left the wickedness of racial segregation wholly untouched. It is an understandable reaction to this spectacle when Christians begin to say: 'These conversions are wholly illusory. This so-called experience of God is simply an illusion. Conversion means that you change your behaviour. Stop supporting segregation, join the struggle for civil rights. That *is* conversion. The rest is mythological framework which can be discarded.' I say this is an understandable reaction, but it is false. The truth is not that the conversion is illusory, but that it is incomplete. You must talk to the pious segregationist by accepting as *the basis* of discussion the knowledge of God in Jesus Christ which he claims, and not by dismissing it as illusion. If a stand against segregation is identified *simpliciter* with conversion to Christ, and failure so to stand is identified with severance from Christ – and this is what some secular interpretations of the Gospel seem to mean – then there is no place to meet, no ground for persuasion, and no place for forgiveness. No one has done more in our time than Reinhold Niebuhr to help us see the importance of this – that if there is no sense of the transcendence of God's will over our particular ethical decisions, then there is no escape from the self-righteousness which ends up by identifying my cause with God's will and my opponent's with the devil.

Listen, for the authentic accents of belief, to these famous words of Abraham Lincoln in the midst of the Civil War, when he had every human reason to identify his cause with God's and appeal to his people to do the same:

> Both (sides) read the same Bible, and pray to the same God; each invokes His aid against the other. It may seem strange that any men should dare to ask a just God's assistance in wringing their bread from the sweat of other men's faces; but let us not judge that we be not judged. The prayers of both could not be answered; that of neither has been answered fully. The Almighty has His own purposes. . . . Fondly do we hope, fervently do we pray, that this mighty scourge of war may speedily pass away. Yet if God wills that it continue until all the wealth piled up by the bondman's 250 years of unrequited toil shall be sunk, and until every drop of blood drawn with the lash shall be paid with another drawn with the sword, as was said 3,000 years ago, so still it must be said: the judgments of the Lord are true and righteous altogether. With malice towards none; with charity for all; with firmness in the right as God gives us to see the right; let us strive on to finish the work we are in. . . .

True Christian involvement in action is marked precisely by that which van Buren's formulation seems to deny, namely by a refusal to identify my programme wholly with God's will, by a humble and penitent recognition that while I must act resolutely in obedience to what I have so far understood of his will, I must always acknowledge my need of forgiveness for persistent transgression, and my need to forgive my adversary who stands with me under the same divine will and the same divine forgiveness.

3> For my third illustration I take a group of experiences from the work of missions. The question we are discussing comes to a sharp focus when you are involved in preaching the Gospel to a non-Christian people; it is the question, What changes of conduct are required by conversion to

Christ? Every Christian would presumably agree that there is no true conversion which does not involve a change of behaviour. But we cannot agree that conversion *is* simply a change of behaviour and nothing else. To accept this would be to fall into the error of which missionaries are often accused – and there is justice in the accusation – the error of legalism. It is true that Christianity has sometimes been preached in a way which in effect identified conversion for practical purposes with the abandonment of whatever appeared to the evangelist to be the major moral evil in the situation – drink, polygamy, cannibalism or some other. An excellent illustration of the problem is to be found in John Taylor's history, *The Growth of the Church in Buganda*.[1] The first missionaries were convinced, as have been most modern western missionaries to Africa, that the abandonment of polygamy was an indispensable element in conversion. A man who did not put away all but his first wife had not been converted and could not be accepted as a member of the Church. But in the minds of some, at least, of the earliest converts there was a different opinion, namely that the essential ethical issue involved in conversion was that of slavery. No one – in their view – was a Christian who had not broken decisively with the whole system of slavery. For the English missionaries this was an issue upon which it was possible to give the Holy Spirit time to act. After all, the primitive Church did not attack slavery outright. Paul did not tell Philemon that he could not remain a Christian while he kept Onesimus as a slave. It took many centuries for the Church to see that slavery was intolerable for the Christian conscience. But the question of polygamy was different; that required a decision now. No man could be a polygamist and a Christian at the same time. The Buganda converts took the converse view of these two issues, but it was the view of the missionaries which prevailed, and in the history of missions in Africa it has been more or less taken for granted that the abandonment of polygamy is

[1] London: SCM Press (1958).

always and at all times an essential mark of conversion. There are some, of whom I am one, who believe this is both wrong on theological grounds and disastrous in missionary practice. I do not doubt for a moment that monogamy is God's will for the human family. But I also have no doubt that a man married in accordance with traditional practice and in good faith to several wives can be truly converted and enter into a personal knowledge of God through Jesus Christ in the fellowship of God's people, and that it is through that knowledge that he can learn how to order his family life. I am sure, incidentally, that this ordering cannot rightly include the act of abandoning women who have been married to him in honesty and good faith according to the custom and conscience of the society in which they have lived. In other words, I deny an absolute identification of conversion with a particular ethical decision in the matter of polygamy. All conversion has an ethical content, but conversion is an event which is more than its ethical implications. To deny this is to leave the order of grace and freedom and to go over into the world of legalism and bondage. True goodness, as the Christian understands it, is the fruit of grace, that is to say, of a personal relationship with God, in whom alone is perfect goodness, and who with unwearying patience deals with men – commanding, sustaining, chastening, forgiving, guiding in a continuous and living intercourse of love. To be converted is to be brought into that personal relationship with God who is the author and ground of my being but who is other than myself and whom – God forgive me! – I am still free to disobey. Simply to identify conversion with a decision to act in a certain way, whether it be in the matter of polygamy, or slavery, or segregation, is to leave the realm of grace for the realm of law.

It may be said that this argument misses the point because van Buren understands Christian faith not simply as an intention to act in a certain way, but also as a *blik*, a point of view in the light of which one forms this intention. This is true and important. It is legitimate and helpful to describe

So Van Buren's statement on intention to act = to God — is new legalism.

the Christian faith in God as a *blik*. It is a way of looking at all experience, a way which is given to us through the whole event of Jesus Christ. With these affirmations one need have no difficulty. What causes the difficulty is the denial with which van Buren couples his affirmation, his persistent denial that this *blik* leads to any knowledge of any reality. We have agreed that it does not lead to the knowledge of observable objects beyond those accessible apart from it. It does not give knowledge of things beyond the frontiers of science. These frontiers are always temporary. In principle they can always be pushed back. The objects of religious knowledge do not lie beyond them. The question, for example, whether there is such a thing as extra-sensory perception must in due course be settled by the methods of experiment and verification which are used by science. This is something beyond the present frontiers of science, but not beyond scientific investigation, and it is possible that in due course the alleged phenomena of extra-sensory perception will be incorporated in the body of accepted scientific knowledge. We are agreed that the question whether or not the Christian *blik* gives knowledge of a reality other than myself is not of the same order as the question whether or not extra-sensory perception is possible.

Where we do not agree is at the point of van Buren's persistent denial that the Christian *blik* gives knowledge of God. This is made clear not primarily by his reluctance to use the word God: in this he could be simply standing in the tradition of the Bible with its unremitting campaign against idolatry. Where his denial of the cognitive function of the Christian *blik* becomes explicit is in his refusal to acknowledge that the command to love God has any meaning which is not equally and fully expressed in the command to love one's neighbour. At this point van Buren denies the central Christian affirmation that through Christ we can know God.

In the next chapter we shall try to look further at what is meant by knowing God. Here I simply sum up the last of the criticisms I have been making of recent attempts to restate the Gospel in terms of a secularized world.

Truly understood, secularization is the present form of the process by which the ontocratic form of society is broken up and men are required to make their own decisions about belief and conduct. As a Christian I see this process of secularization as an extension of the prophetic attack, in the name of the living God, upon all structures of thought, patterns of society, idols whether mental or metal, which claim sacred authority over men. It is a continuation of God's age-long education of man to stand upon his feet and answer his maker, to live the life of responsible personal freedom.

Believing this, I regard the attempt to play down the biblical emphasis upon God as the living God who confronts man and calls for his answer, as thoroughly mistaken. The end of that road could only be that the secular society becomes the conformist society, and eventually the totalitarian society. A secular society in which the traditional authority of social forms is broken needs more and not less of the prophetic spirit which knows the voice of the living God. It has often been said in India, where the emergence of the secular state is so clearly related to the impact of the Christian West upon an ancient ontocratic society, that it needs Christians to keep the secular state truly secular. I think this is true.

Of a secular society, as of a free society, it must be said that the price is constant vigilance. There must be men and women in whom the authentic prophetic spirit is at work, who can speak in the name of the living God, who are ready to be witnesses, if necessary with their blood, to the reality of his rule. If there are not such, the secular society is an easy prey for totalitarian ideologies. The house out of which the old gods have been expelled lies open to new demons.

3 *Sp experienced*

KNOWING GOD

WHAT does it mean to speak of knowing God? This question cannot be evaded in a discussion of religion in an age of secularization. Our criticism of Professor van Buren has centred in his statement that the Christian *blik* is 'non-cognitive', that it does not give knowledge of 'how things are'. In what sense can we speak of 'knowing God'?

There is no doubt that this question presents itself in a new form for this generation. There have been long periods of human history when belief in the existence of God was almost taken for granted. And this is still true in many parts of the world. I have on many occasions talked with extremely primitive people in South India, people who have had no contact with Christianity or with Islam or with the higher Hinduism; I have always found that they were quite simply convinced that the great reality with whom they had to do at every turn, from whom they came and to whom they would have to give account, was God. Let us remember that this conviction is – in some form or other – apparently among the most primitive and basic elements in the human story.

However, there is no doubt that we are in a different situation. Belief in God is no longer, for secularized modern man, a normal part of his mental furniture. As I have already suggested, this does not necessarily mean that the questions which the Gospel puts to modern man are radically different from those of a former time. One must by no means simply identify belief in God, in the sense in which we are now speaking of it, with the response of faith to the revelation of God in Jesus Christ. */These people who say "I believe in God, sir!"*

But there is another side to the matter which is perhaps even more important for our present purpose, namely what one may call the doubt of the believing man. Here we are not speaking of irreligious atheism. This does not present so serious a problem. If a man never takes the trouble to listen attentively to a piece of music we shall not be surprised if he tells you that a Bach fugue means nothing to him. The atheism of the man who has never tried to enter into the religious experience does not present to the believer a very serious problem. Let me speak rather of the problem of faith and unbelief from the point of view of the man who seeks to walk by faith, to worship and to pray. Let me try to look at the problem from within rather than from without. No one who has seriously tried to live the life of faith is, surely, wholly without some experience of the mystery of unbelief. At least there is an extensive litera-ture to testify, if we do not know it already from our own experience, that prayer is not all plain sailing. The prayers of the most devout men and women have been maintained in a continual struggle against blank unbelief, when it seemed that heaven was closed and there was none to answer. The psalms are full of the complaint of faithful men who are tempted to believe that God has abandoned them. In spite of the testimony of Newman, I must confess that I find it hard to believe that any Christian who takes prayer seriously does not have to go through experiences of desolation when it seems that prayer is a meaningless expense of spirit and that there is really no one there, at the other end, so to speak, to hear his words and to receive the outpoured offering of his adoration. And what are we to make of the fact that at the very heart of the Christian proclamation there stands the record that Jesus at the hour of death went through an experience of total dereliction? 'My God, my God, why hast thou forsaken me?' How shall we speak of the knowledge of God in the face of such facts as these? What is this knowledge which can be so totally eclipsed, which can give way to such a desolating sense that there is no one there? What kind of knowledge is it which, even for those who have sought it most diligently, can evaporate into nothingness? It is not just for the unbeliever, but for the honest believer, that this question is so searching. How shall we speak of the knowledge of God in a way which is really honest?

I think we cannot tackle this question without trying to say something, however inadequate, about what we mean by knowing anything. Here, more perhaps than in most other matters, we tend to take over uncriticized the assumptions of our culture, and it is therefore the more important to be aware of these assumptions and of the fact that other assumptions are possible. Our present culture accustoms us to regard as the ideal of knowledge the kind of knowledge which can ultimately be stored in an electronic computor. We are accustomed to regard other kinds of knowledge as being reliable in the measure that they approach that standard. But quite other views can be and are held. One who has absorbed the thought-forms of Hinduism, at least in its central tradition, sees as the ideal and standard of knowledge that which can be attained by abstraction from all the impressions of sense. The data provided by the five senses, so far from being regarded as the foundation of all else, are regarded as basically unreliable and even illusory. The true knowledge by which all else is to be measured is found by withdrawal from them into an inner citadel of pure subjectivity. The language of the Bible introduces us to yet a third view of knowledge. The central use of the verb 'to know' in the Old Testament is its use in respect of the mutual knowledge of persons. It expresses a relationship in which much more is involved than knowledge of facts, of concepts, or of mathematical or logical operations. One of the most significant uses of the verb in the Old Testament is its use to describe the act of love between a man and a woman. There is expressed, if you will, the ideal of knowledge from the biblical point of view – the total mutual self-revelation and surrender of persons to one another in love.

And the Bible repeatedly uses the analogy of the sexual relation to describe the mutual knowledge of God and his people.

It is from within this biblical tradition that I speak if I try to say something of what is meant by the knowledge of God. But I believe that this understanding of knowledge helps us to understand the nature of all knowing, and to understand that the knowledge of God is not unrelated to all our other kinds of knowledge, including that which can ultimately be stored in a computer.[1]

1. In the first place let us note the obvious point that all knowing is a skill. One must learn to know. This is true from the very first beginnings of perception when an infant learns to focus its eyes and to distinguish objects from their background and from the total blur of lights and shades around it. This skill which is acquired by the process of learning and practice contains elements which cannot be specified in any formula which would thenceforth obviate the necessity of learning. The skills involved in riding a bicycle depend for their effectiveness upon laws of motion and gravity which can be stated in terms of formulae which can be fed into a computer. But the availability of these formulae does not eliminate the process of learning necessary to acquire the skill. The same is true at all stages of learning, whether it be in acquiring skill in riding a bicycle or in using a mathematical or logical process. Knowledge does not impose itself upon us – at any stage. It is acquired by being learned, and it is learned by acquiring the skills necessary to carry through the mental operations involved in learning. Knowing is a personal achievement which, in appropriate cases, is rewarded by the gift of a prize. Knowing is an activity of persons.

2. Knowing is an activity of persons in community. This is also true from the first beginnings of knowing in infancy. The earliest knowledge of a new-born baby is knowledge of

[1] Readers of *Personal Knowledge* by Michael Polanyi, London: Routledge (1958), will recognize in what follows my debt to this book.

its mother. As it grows, its knowledge of things around it is knowledge of a world shared with its parents and other members of the family. The names by which it learns to distinguish one thing from another are names learned from them. This communal aspect of learning remains essential from start to finish. All progress in knowledge depends upon the existence of a community of persons who share their experience and who mutually trust one another to accept certain standards. Throughout the whole process there are personal decisions to be made, about which personal conflict may ensue between different scholars. In these conflicts much more is involved than purely intellectual activities. There are involved the total personalities of those concerned. This combination of mutual trust with the readiness for mutual resistance and conflict are part of the stuff without which there can be no advance in knowledge. From beginning to end our knowledge of the world is a shared knowledge; indeed without this communal element we could have no assurance even of the reality of what we think we see and feel. No human being is strong enough to go on asserting the existence of something in face of the unanimous denial of the rest of mankind. If he tries, he is put in a mental hospital. Not only our appreciation of music, of poetry, of architecture and of philosophy, but also our knowledge of the physical world depends upon our participation in a community of persons within which there is at least some real measure of mutual knowledge and trust.

(3) Knowing involves a risk and a commitment. It involves the acceptance, at least provisionally, of beliefs which might be mistaken. One cannot even speak a sentence without accepting provisionally the framework of thought which this language expresses and which is itself the result of the particular history of the people who speak it. One comes to realize this when one is trying to master a language which belongs to a totally different family of languages from one's own – as, for instance, when an Englishman learns to speak

Tamil. The very structure of the language and the use of the words arises from an immensely long experience different at important points from that which has formed the English tongue. And yet one cannot begin to speak without provisionally accepting that framework of thought. As we use words reflectively, we become aware of assumptions underlying them which we had taken over uncritically with the word when we first heard it used. We then use other words in order to try to correct the false assumption, but in order to carry out this critical activity we have to accept for the moment and use uncritically another set of words. There is no way of speaking except by taking these risks. The true seers, the poets and the original thinkers, create new patterns of words and run the risk of writing nonsense. But this is the necessary risk involved in the efforts to know more deeply. The same risk is run by the artists and the composers and the architects who create new patterns of colour or shape or sound, often at the risk of uttering nonsense. But the risk has to be run in order that the possibility may be created for the human community to discern beauty which it had not before discerned. And the same is also true of the great advances in mathematics and the natural sciences. The great scientific advances have been creative and imaginative leaps in which the scientist was taking the risk of being declared wrong. One does not need to be reminded of the fierce controversies which have surrounded the first announcement of some of the great new theories. Science has not advanced by the method of sticking to facts which cannot be contradicted. Quite the opposite. It has advanced by the daring of those who created completely new patterns of thought even when there were still plenty of facts that could be used to refute them.

It is strange that so many scientists, or popularizers of science who are read by laymen like myself, try to suppress this obvious fact and to suggest that scientific theories are simply imposed on the mind of the scientist by facts which cannot be disputed. When I first tried to understand what the theory of relativity was about, I read that the theory had been developed to meet the facts disclosed by the Morley Michelson experiments, which were alleged to demonstrate that the speed of light was identical for two observers travelling at high speeds in opposite directions from or towards the source of the light. I have seen this statement repeated many times since. But it has now apparently been conclusively shown (*a*) that Einstein had never heard of the Morley Michelson experiments when he developed his general theory; (*b*) that these experiments did not give the result required by Einstein's theory; and (*c*) that these experiments have since been repeated many thousands of times with refined instruments and have not yet produced the result required by the theory. The theory of relativity has been validated by the enormous expansion of knowledge and power which it has made possible. But it was not in origin something imposed on the mind of the scientist by so-called facts. It was an imaginative leap, ahead of existing knowledge, the commitment of a great mind to a proposition of which it was possible for excellent scholars to say that it was wrong.[1]

It is therefore wholly erroneous to say, as is often said in discussions about religious knowledge, that real knowledge is only achieved by a scrupulous care in avoiding any possibility either of believing anything which is beyond the evidence or of saying anything which is not entirely clear and immediately verifiable. In fact the extension of knowledge in all realms of human experience is achieved in defiance of these two rules. Anyone is, of course, free to invent games as he wishes and to lay down the rules. But reality, if one may be excused for using the word, is almost by definition that which does not submit to our rules but requires us to submit to its. All the evidence of human experience, the evidence of the greatest of men, the poets, the artists, the scientists and the saints, goes to suggest that knowledge is accessible to those who are ready to keep

[1] Polanyi, *Personal Knowledge*, Ch. 1.

the doors open, to venture beyond what is clear and unquestionable, even if it involves the risk of being mistaken or talking nonsense. It is difficult to read the whole story of the human quest for knowledge without coming to the conclusion that it is more dangerous to be afraid of making a mistake than to be afraid of missing something real. To put it in another way, it is possible to be led astray both by too much faith and by too much doubt, but there can be no question that the active principle in knowing is faith. The ancient word of Anselm is true of much more than theology: one must believe in order to understand.

To say this is not for a moment to deny that doubt and scepticism have an indispensable role to play in the art of knowing. Some facts alleged by religious believers are untrue, some words written under the name of poetry have been nonsense, and some scientific theories have been mistaken. Not to stray outside my own proper field, there is a great deal in the world of religious language and practice which calls for a much more rigorous scepticism than it often gets in religious circles. To be prepared to face sceptical scrutiny is the necessary mark of any belief which is belief in what is real. But scepticism is not the active principle in the advance of knowledge. The active principle is the willingness to go out beyond what is certain, to listen to what is not yet clear, to search for what is hardly visible, to venture the affirmation which may prove to be wrong, but which may also prove to be the starting-point for new conquests of the mind. In the traditional language of Christianity the name for that active principle is faith.

4) However, it is obvious that neither in ordinary speech nor in the speech of the Bible are 'faith' and 'knowledge' synonymous. In many contexts faith is used for a state of mind which may be a preparation for knowledge but certainly falls short of knowledge. A man may be sustained in a long course of difficult research by the faith that he is on a fruitful line and that it will eventually bring results. But the result he expects is something different from the faith

which sustains him: it is assured knowledge, let us say, in principle, knowledge of the kind which could be fed into a computer. No one is going to confuse these two things. And it might seem natural to go on the very common view that the highest role which can be assigned to faith is that it is an element in the achievement of knowledge, but can never be more than that. Where we have to be content with faith, it is simply because knowledge is not available, or because of invincible ignorance.

However, the matter is not quite so simple as that. The result of our scientist's research may be such that in due course it becomes part of what is regarded as assured knowledge. It goes into the textbooks and becomes the basis for further research. Yet, in spite of the fact that it is in this sense regarded as 'knowledge', our scientist knows that it is perfectly possible that in a few years' time it will be superseded as the result of further research. When that happens he will not fight for its retention. It is, in truth, provisional. But if a school of thought were to arise which attacked not his particular findings, but the whole scientific method; if, let us say, due to some unforeseen swing of the political pendulum there should be a demand by government that the medical faculty should begin to teach the Ayur Vedic system of medicine, or that astrology should be introduced as an optional paper for the B.Sc. degree, then our scientist, if he is worth his salt, will fight back. The conviction for which he will fight is not 'knowledge' of the kind that could be fed into a computer. It is faith in the validity of the scientific method over against its predecessors. It is faith in the integrity of the community of scientists to which he belongs and to which he owes loyalty. It is not knowledge. It is not assured in the sense of the 'assured findings' which have passed into the textbooks. But he will fight for it, as he would not fight for the other. If reality is that which has to be reckoned with, which requires us to alter course, which cannot be simply walked through as one walks through a phantom, then it would seem that the not on basis of proof, but freedom to believe — i that scientist fight for.

86 *Honest Religion for Secular Man*

objects of faith may have a higher degree of reality than the objects of our knowledge. It is difficult to deny, unless we are to condemn as irrational the kind of behaviour which we normally applaud as noble, that faith may bring us into contact with reality no less surely than knowledge. Or, to put it in another way, it is difficult to deny there are realities which we *know* by faith.

5. There is one realm where this is obviously true, namely the knowledge which we have of other people. In an earlier chapter I wrote of the distinction between two ways of knowing, knowing an object and knowing another person. This distinction has been made familiar in the writings of Martin Buber, with their sharp reminder of the difference between the relation I-Thou and the relation I-It. The knowledge of an object is achieved by processes of inspection and experiment in which the knowing subject is the only active agent. Knowledge of another person involves the recognition of another centre of decision which it is not in my power to control. True knowledge of that other person – knowledge in the Hebrew sense of the word to which I referred at the beginning of this chapter – can only come as the result of a mutual trust leading to a mutual self-revelation. This is a self-revelation which the other can, if he will, finally withhold. I may even use torture and the threat of death to extract from another some secret about himself, but he can still withhold from me that trust and love which are the substance of personal knowledge. What is true of all knowing is supremely true of the knowledge of another person, that one must believe in order to know. It is possible to learn by observation and even by experiment a great deal about a person. It is possible to use a person, and to discover how he can be used. But to treat the person in this way is to exclude oneself from the possibility of knowing the person as he or she truly is. That knowledge is a matter of self-revelation which depends wholly upon mutual trust, mutual respect, mutual caring.

In the earlier chapter I was at pains to establish the

distinction between the knowledge of things and the knowledge of persons. The course of the present argument is making it clear, I trust, that while there is a distinction, there is no separation. Theology is led away on a false trail when it tries to isolate the personal from the human experience of the impersonal and to found itself exclusively on the personal. In fact all personal relations are achieved within a context in which impersonal factors play also an essential part – institutional, economic, biological factors of all kinds. The attempt to isolate the personal does violence to the facts and produces the kind of misunderstandings which are found, if I may say so, in Emil Brunner's later writings about the Church. The argument of the present chapter seeks to show that knowledge is all of a piece, and that even our knowledge of the kind of facts which can be stored in an electronic computer cannot be understood except as personal knowledge, knowledge which is the achievement of persons, living in a community of persons, and, in a very real sense, living by faith. The mutual knowledge of persons is not something apart from our other knowledge. It is not an exception to the general rule which might be allowed for but which could not govern our basic thinking. It is, on the contrary, the context and the precondition of all knowing. Without it there can be no other kinds of knowledge. The biblical usage in which the primary meaning of the verb 'to know' refers to this mutual knowledge of persons is not an archaeological oddity. It is a profoundly significant witness to the truth about all knowing.

6. In the light of this discussion about knowing in general we must now approach our central question: what does it mean to speak of the knowledge of God? Manifestly, in the first place, our language about knowing God is to be interpreted in terms of what we have described as personal knowledge. To know God is not to know of the existence of an object over and above the sum of objects whose existence is known to unbelievers. Nor is it a kind of knowledge separate from our whole knowledge of the world

of things and persons. Such knowledge is not accessible to us. Even our most intimate personal knowledge of one another is possible only through our sharing together in a common world of things and persons. There is no other personal knowledge available to us. It has been suggested that some kinds of insects communicate with one another by direct psychic means and that this explains the extraordinary order and cohesion of insect communities. We have known of human relationships in which one person had such a psychic power over the other that he could enforce his will almost without the use of explicit speech. But this is not true personal knowledge. Such knowledge is only achieved through sharing together in a common world of things, of experiences, of ideas. *A fortiori* it is only through the shared world of nature and history that we have knowledge of God. It is in, with, and under this shared world of things and persons that we can know God.

But what, then, does it mean to know God? Can we accept the paraphrases which Bishop Robinson gives at this point in his argument? Can we translate the biblical language about man's communion with God into such statements as he uses: 'Reality at its very deepest level is personal'; 'Personality is of ultimate significance in the constitution of the universe'; 'Belief in God is the trust . . . that Love is the ground of our bein, to which ultimately we "come home"'?[1] I do not think we can. It is indeed extremely difficult to know what these statements mean in the context of the Bishop's argument. What does it mean to say that love is the ground of our being, to which we ultimately come home, if one has first denied the existence of the Lover? What is love when there is no lover? Having written off 'the effort to persuade oneself of the existence of a super-Being beyond this world endowed with personal qualities',[2] the Bishop then asks us to perform the more

---

[1] *Honest to God*, John A. T. Robinson, London: SCM Press; Philadelphia: Westminster Press (1963), pp. 48-9.

[2] Op. cit., p. 49.

impossible feat of believing that we 'ultimately come home'
to love.

We cannot persuade ourselves any more of the existence
of God. That era of human history has ended. But neither
can we persuade ourselves of the truth of the very abstract
statements in which Bishop Robinson tries to preserve some
echoes of the Christian faith. There is certainly little in
human experience to assure us of their truth in the face of
the things which seem to deny them. At this point fidelity
to our argument, no less than fidelity to the Gospel, requires
that one moves from the language of argument to that of
testimony. Fidelity to the argument, because one can only
know another person if he makes himself known. If one
could argue from general human experience to the existence
and goodness of God, one would still be, from a biblical
point of view, in the world of unbelief. We cannot argue
ourselves into knowledge of another person. That person
must meet us, and we must learn by speech, action, event,
to know that person in the concreteness and particularity of
his person. The Christian testimony is that God has so
acted, so spoken, so given himself to us in Jesus, that we
know that he loves us, and that that knowledge is constantly
confirmed and enriched through the events of daily life. To
say this is to say something that belongs to a different order
of statement from the statement that ultimate reality is personal, even though the latter might be a legitimate deduc-
tion from the former.

I confess that at this central point I find *Honest to God*
elusive. At some points in the argument, Bishop Robinson
is insisting that the thought of God as another person must
be abandoned as being impossible for modern man. But at
other points he speaks of our need to acknowledge 'the
eternal Thou'. I find it impossible to reconcile these two
positions. This is the central point, as it seems to me, in
the *Honest to God* discussion. 'To believe in God as love,'
says Bishop Robinson, 'means to believe that in pure personal relationship we encounter . . . the deepest, veriest

truth about the structure of reality. This, in face of all the evidence, is a tremendous act of faith. But it is not the feat of persuading oneself of the existence of a super-Being beyond this world, endowed with personal qualities.[1] Perhaps I can state my difficulty with this, by making the obvious point that my personal relations are not pure. Even in loving I injure and am injured. Even in knowing I estrange and am estranged. I need a third party to help me. I cannot find the way alone. It is because he who made me and whose I am, who is indeed the ground of my being, whom I injure in my blundering egotism and from whom I am estranged in my blindness, it is because he has forgiven that I can forgive and be forgiven. It is because he has reconciled us both that my neighbour and I can be reconciled. I learn true love when both my beloved and I know that there is One to whom we both owe an allegiance that has priority over the allegiance we owe each other. It is only in the presence of that Other that we learn step by step what a pure personal relation can be. The Bishop is right in what he affirms, that the eternal *Thou* is met *in, with and under* our experience of other persons and of the natural world; he is wrong when he denies that this eternal Thou is truly other, truly beyond. To remove this otherness is to remove the whole pungency, the whole reality from the Christian experience of God. It is to remove that which makes the whole enterprise of Christian discipleship real, the assurance of dealing with a heavenly Father who is really there, who hears and answers prayer, who forgives and heals, who overrules and corrects – who is *there*.

It follows from Bishop Robinson's position that he does not have to wrestle with the problem of doubt. He quotes Tillich in interpreting theology as being about 'that which concerns us ultimately'. 'A statement is theological', he says, 'not because it relates to a particular being called "God", but because it asks *ultimate* questions about the meaning of existence: it asks what, at the level of *theos*, at

[1] Op. cit., p. 49.

the level of its deepest mystery, is the reality and significance of our life.'[1] It follows from this that there can be
no such thing as doubt in the sense in which we have been
discussing it, nor can there be such a thing as atheism.
Everyone is ultimately concerned about *something*, and
everyone knows something about the mystery of human
existence. Therefore, in the sense in which we are using
terms, everyone in fact believes in God. The agonizing
problem of religious doubt is thus solved at one stroke and
it is not surprising that for many of the most sincerely
religious men and women the publication of this book
brought an immense sense of release. The sigh of relief was
audible throughout the world. Yet we have to ask whether
the release was not achieved too cheaply.

There is indeed a sense in which every man knows God
even if he does not know that he knows him. God is the
ground of our being because he is our creator, sustainer and
Lord. We have no existence except in him. It is he who is
dealing with us all the time. Moreover, as we shall see, what
is called atheism may in fact be a valid attack upon
idolatry masquerading as faith in God. But this does not
mean that we can accept the simple equation 'God' equals
'ultimate concern'. For the believer in God, God is indeed
his ultimate concern, but one cannot reverse the sentence to
read: 'Ultimate concern' equals 'God'. God is no category;
he is the living God, the God of Abraham, of Isaac, of
Jacob, the God and Father of our Lord Jesus Christ. If one
knows God so, knows him in the sense in which the Bible
speaks of knowing him, then one knows also that he is the
ground of all being, and the ground of all who do not
acknowledge him. It is because one knows him as the living
God, that one knows that in pure personal relationship we
encounter the deepest truth about the structure of reality.
It is knowing him which is primary. One can reason from
the reality of God as revealed in Jesus to the primacy of
personal relationships; but the acknowledgment of the

[1] Op. cit., p. 49.

primacy of personal relations is not the same as knowing
God.

This brings me back to the question of doubt. It is obvious
that the existence of God can be doubted, is in fact
doubted, even by believers. This seems to some, I think to
Bishop Robinson, a reason for trying to find some way of
stating religious faith which is not open to doubt. I think
this rests on a wrong concept of knowledge. It rests, that is
to say, upon the conception which dominates our contemporary culture, that the ideal form of knowledge is
knowledge which is proof against doubt. I am arguing that
this is a false ideal of knowledge, and that we are on the
wrong track if we try to describe the knowledge of God in
terms which eliminate the possibility of doubt. For myself
I have to confess that the heart of the whole matter is at the
point from which Bishop Robinson wants to remove our
attention – at the point where I know that I am dealing
with the living God who is, if you like, the eternal Thou, but
who is emphatically not a category but a living personal
being. If this be illusion, then it seems to me that the rest
of the language about ultimate concern, about self-trans-
cendence, about the ground of our being, is robbed of real
meaning. They are phrases which echo an experience whose
substance has disappeared. I am concerned about knowing
God, knowing him as one who is other than myself, as the
Father whom I worship, whose forgiveness I seek, whose
will I desire to know, and from whom I ask those things
that he knows I need. When I so worship and pray it is
not enough for me to remember that arguments can be
found for believing in the ultimacy of the personal. I want
to know whether he is there, and whether he hears me. And
I want to know why it is that, if he is there, it is possible
for me to doubt it. I want to know why he seems to hide
himself. And, to be frank, I cannot accept the solution of
the problem which, as far as I understand them, both Professor van Buren and the Bishop of Woolwich offer me,
namely that no one is there except myself. If it is really

true that I am only talking to myself, even if it be that my
upper storeys are talking to the ground floor, then I would
rather stop. Perhaps I am being crude, but I think the Bible
is crude at this point. The faith which I confess is nothing
at all if it is not faith in one who is other than myself. How,
then, can I doubt that he is there without exposing myself
to the devastating charge that it is all illusion?

7. One must, I think, begin the answer to that question
by looking again at the character of a personal relation. We
know other persons as they manifest themselves through
our physical environment, through sight and sound and
touch. It is by their words and their acts that they reveal
themselves, but that revelation does not go far until it is
mutual. Personal knowledge depends upon mutual trust.
And this trust includes as one essential ingredient respect
for the independence and integrity of the other. If I feel, in
respect of another person, that 'I've got him where I want
him', and can be sure that he has no further surprises in
store for me, then my relation with him falls short of true
mutual personal knowledge. The greater and richer the
personality of the other, the more certain is it that, even in
a lifetime of contact, my knowledge of him will not be
exhaustive. He will still have surprises to spring which make
me realize that there was more to him than I understood.
In true personal relations, the other always remains free.
Even in the most intimate of such relations, in marriage at
its very best, there is, and there ought to be, more on each
side than can be fully known to the other. Each person
remains free, with depths of consciousness, of memory, of
desire, and of imagination which the other can never completely grasp and must always respect. True personal knowledge is threatened by the possessiveness which is not willing
to accept this, but which lusts for the kind of relationship
in which one can take the other for granted, in which
everything is under control, in which there are no more
unfathomed depths and no more surprises.

If this is true in the mutual knowledge of men and

women, it must certainly be true of man's knowledge of God. Man can know God only in so far as God manifests himself in events which are accessible to man's observation and which are interpreted as God's doing. These events will enable man to know God in so far as man grasps them as occasions for trusting God and obeying him. Without this response there is no personal knowing. But this knowing can never be complete. 'We know in part.' The full richness of God's being must far transcend all that we have grasped by grasping these events as the disclosure of his character. We must be ready for surprises, be constantly aware that the God who is so revealed is also hidden; that a lifetime is not enough to fathom the depths of his being. We must, to use the biblical imagery, be pilgrims, always ready to move on, to leave even the most hallowed place, to take down even the sanctuary where God has shown himself to us, and move on. But we do not want to do this. We want the religion that we have, rather than the risky faith that God has somewhere more in store for us. The story of the children of Israel in the wilderness is the mirror which the Bible holds up to us to show us the whole story of human religion.

We know God as he reveals himself to us. There is no other way to the knowledge of persons. He reveals himself in what he does. We cannot forecast or control it. Suddenly we know that he was there, in that bush burning in the desert, in that storm sweeping aside the waters and making a path for the escaping slaves, in that man hanging upon a gallows. That was the moment when we saw, and we go back to it; we must go back to it again and again to renew the vision. The whole believing community goes back again and again to the place where the disclosure was made. The words and acts of Jesus are read and expounded, his baptism is re-enacted for each believer, his death and resurrection are shown forth again in the breaking of bread and the sharing of the cup. These acts, repeated, formalized so that they may become the common possession of all races and all generations, constitute the visible substance of religion. By them the believing community relives the moment of revelation, renews its participation in it, reaffirms its faith in its truth. These are the visible forms by which the knowledge of God is expressed and renewed.

But they can also become something else. They can become a place where we try to escape from the living God. Religion can become the enemy of faith. The forms of religion can become an occasion for idolatry. That is to say, we can come to regard them as the means by which a certain aspect of life, that which is called religious, is handled with safety and propriety, is kept under proper control and management. But the living God, he whose self-revealing these religious forms express and commemorate, is not susceptible of being kept under proper control and management. He is free, with depths beyond all human comprehension of creativity, resourcefulness, goodness. He is the Lord, who is in fact holding in his hands the whole secular life of man, active and sovereign in that secular life. He can only be known in a continually fresh exposure to and encounter with his infinite creativity in the life of the world. The forms of religion can be used as a means of protection against this exposure. They can become a cave where one escapes from the presence of the living God. One can almost say that the central strand of the Old Testament story is the struggle of the prophet to speak the word of the living God in relation to the secular events of his time, and against the religion of his time. The word of God in the mouth of the prophet is always the summons to recognize and obey the will of God in the actual events of contemporary history. It is always a summons to move on. The prophetic understanding of the life of faith is unforgettably expressed in the words of the ninth chapter of the Book of Numbers:

> On the day that the tabernacle was set up, the cloud covered the tabernacle, the tent of the testimony; and at evening it was over the tabernacle like the appearance of

fire until morning. So it was continually; the cloud covered it by day, and the appearance of fire by night. And whenever the cloud was taken up from over the tent, after that the people of Israel set out; and in the place where the cloud settled down, there the people of Israel encamped. At the command of the LORD the people of Israel set out, and at the command of the LORD they encamped; as long as the cloud rested over the tabernacle, they remained in camp. Even when the cloud continued over the tabernacle many days, the people of Israel kept the charge of the LORD, and did not set out. Sometimes the cloud was a few days over the tabernacle, and according to the command of the LORD they remained in camp; then according to the command of the LORD they set out. And sometimes the cloud remained from evening until morning; and when the cloud was taken up in the morning, they set out, or if it continued for a day and a night, when the cloud was taken up they set out. Whether it was two days, or a month, or a longer time, that the cloud continued over the tabernacle, abiding there, the people of Israel remained in camp and did not set out; but when it was taken up they set out. At the command of the LORD they encamped, and at the command of the LORD they set out; they kept the charge of the LORD, at the command of the LORD by Moses.[1]

The tent of meeting, the place where God's glory dwells and where God meets with man, the place of religion, has to be moved on as God's people follow their Lord through the world. The temptation to settle down permanently has to be resisted. Today's religion can become the enemy of tomorrow's faith. The pillar of cloud moves on. The same God who gave his presence and his blessing, also withdraws them. This desolating experience has been common to men of faith in all ages. One might almost call it the pattern of the life of faith. The man who has known the life of prayer as an experience of strength and consolation, finds that prayer has become a desolation and a desperate struggle against unbelief. From the brightness of an assured experience of God he finds himself in the deepest darkness of

[1] Numbers 9.15-23 (RSV).

the soul apparently alone. I have noticed in the experience
of many new converts that the early steps of their pilgrimage
are marked by this kind of brightness. God is near, prayer is
answered, everything is clear and sure. But then the early
brightness seems to fade and everything is dark and prayers
seem to be unanswered. I have known a missionary in the
full maturity of a deeply fruitful career come and confess
that prayer had become an utter desolation and that even
participation in the Eucharist had become a duty to be
fulfilled with a dry and cold heart. And the very same
pattern is given for all time in the story of the ministry of
Jesus, where at the beginning everything is bright, the sick
are healed and the hungry are fed. But when they come
back for more, they are met with words hard to understand
about bread that does not perish. The sky steadily darkens
until he whose coming was like the rising of the sun, dies in
darkness with the cry of desolation on his lips.

It is not that God is no more. It is that he has moved on.
This desolation has to be accepted as the only gateway
to renewed communion. The man of prayer must learn to
accept humbly and believingly the discipline of desolation
with the prayer 'If it be thy will, let this cup pass from me;
nevertheless not my will but thine be done.' The struggling
believer must learn to walk by faith, not by sight. The
disciple must learn to know the presence of the risen Lord.
The path of faith runs between the two abysses of idolatry
and atheism, between the desire to have God's presence as a
manageable reality among the forms of human business, and
the abandonment of all belief in God. What is called atheism
may sometimes be in truth a protest against idolatry; it is
wise for Christians to remember that the earliest Christians
were called atheists. But there is an atheism which is
simply the abandonment of faith and which ends in that
conformity to the world which is damnation.

To know God, the living God, means to live in the constant expectancy of what is new, yet in the constant certainty
that nothing which happens can contradict the reality of

what has been revealed. This is what the Bible means by
the faithfulness of God. It is the personal knowledge of one
whom we know to be utterly consistent and yet endlessly
original. It means living a life of faith, which is a continuous
exposure to the endlessly new doings of this faithful God
in the affairs of the secular world. In Evelyn Underhill's
phrase, it means total commitment to the will of God as it
is disclosed in circumstances. In Dietrich Bonhoeffer's
phrase, it means enduring reality before God. It means a
life in which the business of living and the business of praying are intimately woven together, in which all our acts are
simply acted prayers to God for the doing of his will, and
all our prayers look for their answers in the affairs of the
secular world. It is a life whose character is perfectly expressed in the paradox of a portable sanctuary, a tent of
meeting which could be carried on pilgrimage. It is neither
a life without a sanctuary, nor a life gathered in static order
round a fixed shrine. It is a life in which we meet God continually, but never in the same place; in which our meeting
with him is a summons to go out into the place where he is
not, and in which his meeting is prepared for us in the place
where we have gone out, often not knowing whither we
went. It is a life which can be described both as following
Christ and as abiding in Christ, because he is himself the
way.

The life of faith is a continually renewed victory over
doubt, a continually renewed grasp of meaning in the midst
of meaninglessness. I hope to have shown grounds for
believing that, just by this fact, it authenticates itself as a
true contact with reality. I know no place where it is more
truly expressed than in the last poem written by Bonhoeffer from his prison. I venture to think that one understands the real faith of Bonhoeffer better by listening to this
poem, than by trying, as the Bishop of Woolwich seems to
do, to squeeze his thought into a mould of the thought of
Paul Tillich who is really saying the precise opposite of
Bonhoeffer. Bonhoeffer speaks of the picture of himself

which others have given him, calm, cheerful and firm. He contrasts it with the knowledge he has of himself, 'restless, longing and sick like a bird in a cage'. Then he goes on:

Who am I? This or the other?
Am I one person today and tomorrow another?
Am I both at once? A hypocrite before others,
And before myself a contemptibly woebegone weakling?
Or is something within me still like a beaten army,
Fleeing in disorder from victory already achieved?

Who am I? They mock me, these lonely questions of mine.
Whoever I am, Thou knowest, O God, I am Thine![1]

All knowing is an adventure. Knowing God is the supreme adventure which takes us out beyond everything that we can know, to the place where we cannot even answer the question 'Who am I?' The man of faith knows that he does not know, but knows that he is known. 'Thou knowest, I am thine.' It is an utter trust in One who is not myself but who is utterly trustworthy. It is an assured hope that in the end it will be clear that this is all that matters. As another famous prisoner has said: 'Now we see through a glass darkly, but then face to face: now I know in part, but then I shall know as I am known.'

[1] Dietrich Bonhoeffer, *Letters and Papers from Prison*, London: SCM Press (1956), p. 165 (Fontana edition, Collins); New York: Macmillan.

BEING GOD'S PEOPLE

THE Bible begins the story of salvation by telling how God called Abraham to leave his home and his people, and apparently also his ancestral gods, and to become a pilgrim, and how he promised that through Abraham and his descendants blessing would come to all the nations. From the very beginning the end in view is the blessing of all mankind and in Old Testament use the word blessing means the fullness of God's favour given to men in this life. There is in view from the beginning an end which is both universal in range and secular in character. But Abraham himself is a pilgrim. He has, as the New Testament emphatically points out, 'no inheritance in the promised land, not even a foot's length'. The father of the faithful was a dweller in tents 'who looked for a city whose builder and maker is God'.

This picture of the life of God's people, made vivid and personal in the figure of Abraham, is in the background all through the Bible, providing in each age the standard against which current practice is tested. It is to this picture that the prophets appeal when they see Israel settling down to a way of life in which the God of Abraham is invoked as if he was just one of the local baals whose business it was to protect his own worshippers. The natural man likes his religion nailed down in one place, accessible when required, and a god who will protect him provided the recognized rules are kept. Israel constantly misunderstood God's calling and God's covenant in this way. But that *is* a misunderstanding. The true sons of Abraham – this is the prophetic tradition right through the Bible – are those

who know that they were not called for their own sake, but
for something far more majestic, for the work of the doing
of God's will, and the hallowing of his name and the coming
of his kingdom upon all mankind. They therefore know
themselves to be a pilgrim people who have here no permanent quarters.

The same is true in the New Testament. Jesus does not
simply call men for themselves. He calls them and sends
them. 'I chose you, and ordained you that you should
go . . . ,' says Jesus to his apostles, according to St John;
and again: 'As the Father sent me, so send I you.' The
Church is portrayed in the New Testament as a body of
men and women chosen and sent. Peter and Andrew and
James and John are not portrayed as mystics seeking the
true religion and finding it in the teachings of Jesus. They
are rather shown as men picked by a commander for an
expedition, a task force rather than a study group or a
holy club. It is very significant that, according to St Mat-
thew, Jesus' great sermon is given to those whom he has
already chosen and called to himself. It is not the address
of a teacher seeking to attract those who are interested in
his teaching; it is rather the briefing of select troops by a
commanding officer.

The Church, like the old Israel, has constantly forgotten
this. It has listened to the words 'Come unto me', but not
listened to the words 'Go – and I am with you'. It has
interpreted election as if it meant being chosen for special
privilege in relation to God, instead of being chosen for
special responsibility before God for other men. It has
interpreted conversion as if it was simply a turning towards
God for purposes of one's own private inner religious life,
instead of seeing conversion as it is in the Bible, a turning
towards God for the doing of his will in the secular world.
It has understood itself more as an institution than as an
exhibition. Its typical shape in the eyes of its own members
as well as of those outside has been not a band of pilgrims
who have heard the word 'Go', but a large and solid

building which, at its best, can only say 'Come', and at its worst says, all too clearly, 'Stay away'.

The fact that the Church has thus been misunderstood is widely recognized by Christians today. I think that some of the attempts to correct this misunderstanding are themselves in need of criticism. But I want first to say something more about the way in which we are today, in the context of universal secularization, being made aware of this misunderstanding. I hope that in this way we may see better what it means to be the Church in a secularized society.

I begin with the fact, to which we do not usually give enough attention, that the period in which our thinking about the Church received its main features was the period in which Christianity had practically ceased to be a missionary religion. The rise of Islam and the consolidation of its power right across North Africa and in the Middle East had the effect of isolating Western Christendom from any real contact with the ancient cultures of India and the Far East, and from the peoples of Sub-Sahara Africa. The Eastern Churches, except for that of Russia, found themselves in the position of tolerated minorities which could exist only by refraining from challenging the faith of Islam. Christianity was the folk religion of a diminishing minority of the world's peoples, squeezed into a smaller and smaller part of the western peninsulas and islands of the Eurasian continent. It was in this period, when the dimension of the ends of the earth had ceased to exist as a practical reality in the minds of Christians, that the main patterns of churchmanship were formed. The congregation was not a staging post for world mission but a gathering place for the faithful of a town or village. The ministry was not understood in terms of leadership in mission but in terms of guardianship of those already in the fold. Theology was not concerned so much to state the Gospel in the terms of non-Christian cultures, as with the mutual struggle of rival interpretations of the Gospel. Church history was taught not as the story of missionary advance in successive encounters of the Gospel with different forms of human culture and society, but rather as the story of the doctrinal and other conflicts within the life of the Church. To put it in one sentence, the Church had become the religious department of European society rather than the task force selected and appointed for a world mission.

We are familiar with the fact that, during the last few centuries, the vision of a world missionary task has been recovered, and in the nineteenth and twentieth centuries the Church has become for the first time a worldwide community. This astounding chapter in the history of the Church is still so recent that we do not see it in proportion. Moreover, as I wrote in an earlier chapter, western man is at the moment going through a period of acute embarrassment about his Christian past which makes him unwilling to recognize the place that missions have had, and still have, in the making of modern history.

As an interesting example of this, I might refer to the massive volume reporting the UNESCO conference of 1962 on Education in Africa. At a time when something like 85 per cent of all the school children in that continent were in mission schools, this volume contrives to provide a survey of the total situation without conveying the impression that such a thing as a mission school exists.

There is an interesting psychological study waiting to be undertaken some time. Why was western European man in the mid-twentieth century so eager to export every sort of technical assistance to his former colonial territories and at the same time so embarrassed about the fact that the foundations upon which almost all these programmes of technical assistance had to be built had been laid by Christian missions in the previous one hundred years?

For our present purpose the important point is this. Until the last few decades, this missionary movement, though it had its roots in the life of the Churches, was something distinct from them which scarcely challenged the ordinary assumptions upon which church life was carried on. It is only very recently that theologians, for example, have begun to question the whole traditional doctrine of the Church from a missionary angle. It is only recently, I believe, that scholars have drawn attention to the fact that the classic Reformation documents define the marks of the Church without any reference whatever to its missionary task. It is still true in some parts of Europe that a man cannot be ordained by the Church for foreign missionary service, because one of the indispensable conditions for ordination is a call by a settled congregation. It is only now, in fact since the second world war, that most of the European Protestant Churches are setting about the task of recognizing in their formal documents and structures the fact that world mission is one of the marks of the catholic Church and not an amiable hobby for a handful of ageing enthusiasts.

I draw your attention at this moment, in parenthesis, to the fact that these beginnings of a recovery of a biblical doctrine of the Church as a missionary community are intimately related to the process of secularization. The relationship is complex and I am not sure that I understand it. On the one hand, this biblical understanding could not be recovered until the identification of Church and society in western Europe had been broken. The process of secularization, by which the sacral unity of the Christendom society has been broken and the Church has been set in a new relation with society, has been the pre-condition for the recovery of a biblical, that is to say, a pre-Constantinian, understanding of the Church as a missionary community. On the other hand, the experience of western missionaries working in pagan sacral societies and finding themselves, to their own surprise, to be agents of secularization, has helped older Churches of the western world to recover a missionary doctrine of the Church itself.

In order to forestall possible misunderstandings, let me say that in speaking of a missionary understanding of the Church, I do not advocate the belief that the Church has a merely functional character, that it is merely a means to an end. As I understand the New Testament, the Church can never be so regarded, for it is itself the place where we enjoy, now, fellowship with God through the Holy Spirit. It is even now God's family where we are to be at home. But it is so in what one must call a provisional and anticipatory sense, in a sense which looks towards fulfilment of God's purpose for all men. The Church is thus neither a mere instrument, nor is it an end in itself. It is a foretaste, a first-fruit, which makes us long for the full harvest. It is even now the place where we have joy and peace through Christ, but it is not the place where we merely enjoy these for ourselves; they are for all men, because Christ is for all men. They are the foretaste of the banquet to which he has invited all.

Talk about the Church as a missionary community has become rather common. But most of it has left untouched the centre of the Church's life. It is only within very recent years that the light of a missionary doctrine of the Church has been turned steadily upon the local congregation. This has provoked a process of self-examination and self-criticism which promises to be exceedingly fruitful, but which at the same time has already proved to be difficult and even dangerous just because it comes so close to the centre of the Church's life.

I have said that in the New Testament the Church is depicted as a body of people chosen by God and trained and empowered for a missionary task. It is a task force which exists not simply for the sake of its members, which would be absurd, but for the sake of the doing of God's will in the world. The visible structures of church life which we have inherited from the *corpus Christianum* of mediaeval Europe do not correspond very obviously to that description. The reasons for this are not difficult to explain. When the barbarian tribes accepted the Christian faith under the leadership of their chiefs and were baptized *en masse*, what was needed was a place in each community where the whole population could gather together for worship and for instruction in the new faith. There had to be a church building in the centre of each town or village. The visible centre of the Church's life became a place which truly expressed the divine invitation 'Come unto me', but which could not in the same sense express the divine command 'Go - and I am with you'. There was nowhere to go. The whole community was baptized, and the great pagan world was out of reach and out of sight.

There are some places in the world – not many – where this pattern is still valid, in some of the South Pacific islands, for example, where church and society are coterminous, a single *corpus Christianum*. But there the pagan world, though out of sight, has not been out of mind. The Church in Apia, West Samoa, is like a typical village church from England. But it looks out across the harbour, and from it hundreds of young Samoans have been dedicated and sent out to bring the Gospel to every part of the South Pacific, sometimes at the cost of martyrdom. There are other places where the pattern has never been valid, where the Christian community has never been anything but a small handful in a great pagan society. But in most of Europe it was valid once and is so no longer. In the great majority of European towns and villages the church building is no longer the centre of a Christian society. It is a place to which a small minority of the people who desire these things may repair for worship, teaching and fellowship. It is not a place of training for the penetration and occupation of a foreign society. It is not an instrument of mission. It says 'Come', and there are some who accept the invitation; it does not say 'Go'. It may conceivably support missions, but it is not itself a mission.

To understand how this has happened means to understand the process of secularization at the point which is most sensitive and most critical for the life of the Church. The Church was the centre of the mediaeval town because the Christian religion provided the over-arching ideas within which all the different areas of human life were understood and managed. This is no longer so. The different areas of human thought and life constitute different worlds, governed by concepts of their own. Men may be neighbours in the same town and yet live effectively in two different worlds which hardly meet. If they cultivate adjacent garden plots they may perhaps share for an hour or two a week the single world of horticulture; but if, like the growing multitudes that inhabit new housing developments, they live in apartments, even that is denied them. Their conversation is by telephone, their entertainment by radio and television, their visits are by motor-car, and if they have a lift they do not even meet their neighbours on the staircase. Locality has been abolished. Neighbourhood is no longer a word that refers to a place. Man is no longer a neighbour; he is at best the point of intersection of two or three unrelated worlds.

What can the parish church be in this new concrete city? Even if its spire is still discernible between the cliffs of concrete, glass and stainless steel, and the cross on top distinguishable amid the forest of television aerials, what can it be except the centre of another little, separate world for those who have the special interest called religion.

It is in this new situation into which the process of secularization has thrust us that the sharpest questions have been posed about the traditional structures of congregational life. The structure which we have inherited appears to be neither relevant to the life of a secularized society, nor true to the biblical picture of the Church as a missionary community. What does it mean, in terms of the local congregation, to be God's pilgrim people in a secularized world?

Let me begin by recalling the basic truth which is embodied in the traditional form of the local congregation. It is that the Church is a congregation and not a segregation. In a mediaeval village, the church, standing in the centre of the total human community, is the visible sign of the fact that the Church is for all men whatever their status, gifts or tastes. It is not a private club for those who are religious by temperament; it is the place where all men, simply as men, are to be at home together because it is their Father's house. It is the visible sign and first-fruit of Christ's promise, 'I, if I am lifted up from the earth, will draw all men to myself.' It represents the concern of the Church for every man simply as man. It is the place where neighbours are made brothers.

That pattern still has validity wherever the local community remains the fundamental form of human relationships, even where there has never been a *corpus Christianum*. In a South Indian village, for instance, the local community *is* the human community. Your neighbour who lives in the next-door house is also the man you meet at work, in your leisure, on holidays and on work days. And even though Christians may be a small minority, the church stands in the village as a visible invitation to the whole community. This is even more so in my own experience, where the congregation does not yet have a building of its own. In hundreds of villages where the congregation is too poor to build a church, worship takes place out in the street or in the shade of a tree. One administers the sacraments and preaches the word to a group of believers surrounded by a wider circle of those who do not yet believe, but for whom also Christ came. One speaks to all, and the words spoken to the Church are heard by those outside. And the Church grows, because those who come merely to listen or even to scoff, stay to learn more and finally take the step forward to join the group in the middle. One sees the Church then as something living and moving, as the visible form of the action of the Holy Spirit in drawing men of all kinds to Christ. Just because of the absence of a protecting wall, the Church can sometimes be saved from thinking of itself as a society which exists for its members; it is reminded that it exists because Christ died for all and seeks all. Here the words 'come' and 'go' are both heard. I have very often found in my visits to these village congregations that the men and women who were baptized on one visit are, on the next, the ones who are standing as sponsors for others. They have taken it for granted that the first thing a new Christian does is to go and tell others. Thus the Church grows spontaneously. It is itself the mission, the embassage of Christ sent to all men in his name, *going* in order to bid men *come*, *coming* in order to be *sent*, a gathering and a sending which is for all men.

But even in this relatively simple situation the Church is never simply a congregation. It is, in fact, also a segregation, because its character is given not only by the Gospel it proclaims, but also by the people who actually belong. In the example I have given the members are normally drawn from one or two of the lower castes. Others are invited, but they will probably not come. Even here there are several worlds in one place, and each of these worlds has to be taken seriously. It is not enough for the Church to put up a notice 'all are welcome'. God's apostolate is a more costly business than that. Mission is not just church-extension. There is a *kenosis*, a self-emptying involved. The corn of wheat has to fall into the ground and die. Let me illustrate.

One of the greatest missionaries of all time was the Italian Robert de Nobili, who went to Madura in South India in 1605 as a member of the Portuguese mission there. He found himself part of a mission community outside the city, consisting of the foreign priests and a handful of converts from the outcaste communities. It was not long before he realized that this mission station was not really in India at all. It was an outpost of Portugal, and the converts who had attached themselves to it had really been lifted out of India and put down inside the Portuguese compound wall to become imitation Portuguese Christians. An Indian Christian Church did not yet exist, and there was no hope whatever that the cultured Brahmins of Madura would ever accept the invitation addressed to them to join the only Christian congregation visible to them. De Nobili decided that this was not what he had come for. The corn of wheat must fall into the ground. To the indignation of his colleagues he abandoned the mission station, put on the dress of a Brahmin, and disappeared into the precincts of the great temple of Meenakshi in Madura. There he became the first European to master the Tamil and Sanscrit languages, and to study the sacred literature of Hinduism. He lived as a Brahmin who belonged to Jesus Christ. He *was* the beginnings of an Indian Christian Church. Before long a considerable company of devout and learned Brahmins joined him and were baptized. There was created out of this single corn of wheat something which had never existed before, a truly Indian Christian Church, the first-fruit of India for Christ.

But this had been accomplished at the cost of a segregation on the basis of caste. The established ecclesiastical authorities bitterly attacked him and in the end his experiment was condemned by Rome. They had reason on their side. Is not the Church a congregation wherein *all* men are to be at home together? How can we tolerate caste distinctions in the Church? When Protestants in the eighteenth century repeated De Nobili's method they built up strong Christian Churches in South India, but they bequeathed to the nineteenth and twentieth centuries the problem of caste division in the Church. We are right to condemn racial segregation in the Church of America today. But would there have been a Martin Luther King if from the beginning the only form of Christian fellowship available to Negroes had been as minorities in white congregations? Could the marvellous fruit which we recognize today as Negro Christianity, which has so much that white Christianity lacks, have ever been produced if there had not been built up from the beginning strong Negro Christian congregations? We are in the presence here of a tension in the very nature of the Church which has not been sufficiently recognized. It is expressed in classic form once and for all in the fact that St Paul devoted much of his immense spiritual resources in the early stages of his apostolate to fighting for the independence of the gentile churches over against the Church in Judea, and finally gave his life for

their unity with the Church in Judea. He would not have
the mission to the gentiles interpreted as mere Judean
church extension. The corn of wheat who is Christ himself
must fall into the gentile soil in Corinth or in Antioch and
bring forth its own fruit, a kind of Christian life which will
not be a simple reproduction of Judean Christianity, but
will be a fresh showing forth of the infinite riches of Christ.
But, this battle having been won, he gives the closing years
of his ministry to the knitting up of bonds of mutual love
and service between the gentile and the Jewish congregations, and finally gives his life for the fulfilment of that
mission of reconciliation.

The Church is a congregation, set to draw all men of
whatever kind into one family. But it is also a mission sent
to the nations, that is to say, sent to men not as isolated
individuals, but to men in the full reality of their cultural,
social, economic life as men. For the fulfilment of that
mission it is not enough to say 'Come – all are welcome'.
It is also necessary to go, to leave the establishment behind,
to make daring experiments in seeking to learn what it
means to live the life of Christ in every one of the idioms
and patterns of the myriad human communities. It is necessary that the corn of wheat fall into the ground in order
that the particular fruit of *that* ground may be brought to
perfection for Christ. But yet again, all the fruit is to be
brought into one store. The variety is for the sake of the
unity of the Body of Christ that each may serve not itself
but the whole. This going and coming, this scattering of the
seed and gathering of the fruit, is the very life of the Church
when it is true to its proper nature.

I hope that this journey through South India and Galatia
has prepared us to come back with some new insights to
the Church in the concrete city. What does it mean for the
Church to be both the *congregation* of God and the *mission*
of God in today's secularized, fragmented society? One can
begin with a negative statement. Locality can no more be
the sole basis of congregation. For secularized urban man,

even more than for his predecessors, to live in the same place does not mean to inhabit the same world. Not because we have forgotten that the Church is a congregation and not a segregation, but because we remember it, we have to say that the local church can no longer be the sole definitive form of the Church's existence. I say 'the *sole* definitive form', and I shall come back later to a more positive statement about the local church. But for the moment let me stress only this point. The Church must be where men are, speak the language they speak, inhabit the worlds they inhabit. This is the simplest of missionary principles. In obedience to it, Christians are reaching out in new forms of presence, trying to manifest the reality of the life of Christ in the many varied idioms of the worlds which men inhabit. There are 'cells' in factories and in offices. There are evangelical academies and professional groups based upon them. There are specialized lay ministries in which Christians share but which they do not control, to alcoholics, narcotic addicts, juvenile delinquents. There are concerted efforts to bring Christian faith to bear on key points of decision-making in municipal or national life. But these missionary experiments have, until recently, left untouched the position of the local congregation as the definitive form of the Church, the place where the word is preached, the sacraments dispensed, and godly discipline administered. These other activities have been seen rather as non-ecclesiastical or at best para-ecclesiastical activities which were the outworks of the Church rather than its main structure, the scouting parties rather than the main column.

These assumptions are now being questioned, and rightly so. With the Bible in our hands we must ask, 'Is the Church only truly the Church when it is in camp, and not when it is on the march? Is mission not as truly churchly as congregation? Are these goings forth, these self-emptyings, these fallings into the ground, not as truly of the life of the Church as the settled local congregation? Should these not also have at their heart the ministry, the word and the sacraments as truly and fully as the other? When we use the word ecclesiastical only for the settled and not for the experimental, only for the congregational and not for the apostolic, are we faithful to the Bible? Or are we putting the traditions of men in place of the word of God?'

Let me again illustrate from Indian experience. In India, as in the greater part of Asia and Africa, modern missions began with the legacy of a tradition which separated mission from Church. In the majority of cases the work of preaching the Gospel, instructing new converts and shepherding new congregations was entrusted to unordained agents of the mission. A native Church with its own ministry came later. One began as a mission and later graduated to the status of a Church with an ordained ministry. Today that is being questioned. Why should not the new congregations be recognized as truly the Church from the very beginning? Why should we not do as St Paul did and ordain from among the very first converts men who will be their ministers to dispense to them the word and sacraments? Why do they have to spend years in the position of a sort of out-station before graduating to full churchly status? Does one only become truly the Church when one settles down and ceases to move forward? Out of such questionings have come experiments which, in my own judgment, convincingly demonstrate that the Church can be a true leaven in society, a spontaneously expanding fellowship with its own power to penetrate and grow, even in the difficult conditions of modern India. These new congregations are not extensions of the existing ones, dependent on them for the essentials of their life in Christ. They are new creations, new births, linked in fellowship and mutual caring with the old, but having their own standing before God and their own access to the means of grace.

The same principles must surely be applicable to the attempt to penetrate the multiple worlds of modern secularized society with the Gospel. Groups of Christians who are seeking to discover and to manifest what the will of

God is for the life of man in these several forms of human community, must be acknowledged as true congregations. They should be able in the context of their discipleship as men in industry, in politics, in administration or whatever it is, to experience and express the fullness of what life in Christ means. It should be possible for them to have the full ministry of word, sacrament and fellowship as the centre of their common life while they seek to discover what God wills for their factory, their profession, their university. In my own experience in South India, the logic of this argument led us to ordain to the ministry men who belonged to the village and continued to earn their living as labourers, farmers or teachers. This meant that the new congregations were acknowledged from the beginning as truly the Church of God, responsible to God for letting the light of Christ shine in their village and beyond. They were not simply out-stations responsible to someone else. Should we not also consider whether something of the same kind ought not to be the pattern in a modern urban society? Should not these groups in industry, in the professions, in political life, have their own ministry and sacraments, just as is already done in the case of many universities and schools? This would mean the development of a non-professional ministry, exercised by men who continued to fulfil their secular callings as foremen, managers, doctors, or whatever it was, and this not (as is often wrongly thought) because of a shortage of clergy, but out of respect to the missionary character of the Church. It is out of recognition of the fact that the Church does not discharge its mission to the world by simply saying 'Come'. There may even be a fine church building ably staffed and with splendid activities, but even so it is not enough to say 'Come'. It may be that there are human communities geographically close to the church but spiritually far from it, where men's commitments are made, where they belong together in their daily work, where they are really neighbours in a much more than merely local sense. The Church cannot simply

say to men in these human communities 'Come, leave that
behind for a while, and join this other religious community'.
This might simply mean inviting men to leave their real
responsibilities behind for a while and to engage in activities
which did not touch them at the point where God is to be
served. Rather the Church must be ready to say to its
members 'Go into that community and for Christ's sake give
yourself to it', so that *there*, in the midst of its daily secular
decisions, God's will may be done.

When Bishop Wickham started the Sheffield Industrial
Mission there were already plenty of congregations in that
city. All of them were ready to welcome anybody from the
steel mills who cared to come in. But Wickham saw that
this was not enough. The steel workers were a community
effectively outside the Christian community. It was not
enough to invite them to come in. It was not enough to
send scouting parties into the mills to invite them. There
had to be something more costly. The corn of wheat had to
fall into the ground and die. The mission had to leave the
settled congregation behind and disappear, so to say, into
the mill, ready for many years to be present as learners and
servants and witnesses, until God the Holy Spirit should –
if he were pleased to do so – take their presence and make
it the occasion for a new creation, for the appearing of a
community within the steel mills which would be the
authentic first-fruit of Christ's kingdom in the steel mills.

I have said that we must be ready to acknowledge communities of Christians within different sectors of human
culture, industry, leisure and so on as truly congregations.
The local congregation cannot, in the conditions of our
secularized world, be considered the one definitive form of
the visible Church. But this does not mean that the local
congregation no longer has significance. The place where
men live, where their homes and children are, where some
at least of their leisure time is spent, is also a world which
must be taken seriously. Indeed there may be a very special
responsibility laid upon the Church to create a true com-

munity out of mere physical propinquity in, for example, a modern apartment development where each family lives its private life and there is no natural community at all. My own present experience of living in a new apartment block on the outskirts of Geneva leads me to think that one of the great tasks of the Church in such a situation may be just this – to create the basis for human community where no natural basis exists. But in this situation also, it is not enough for the Church simply to erect a building and say 'Come'. The starting-point is not 'Come', but 'Go', go out to be simply at the service of people in their ordinary human needs and try with them to see in concrete detail what God's will is for the common life of such a neighbourhood. It is out of the human contact that such humble service creates, that the possibility arises that the Holy Spirit will take some deed or word of ours and use it to draw men to Christ, so that they hear him say 'Come'.

One implication of this must be stated. It is that, in the conditions of a secularized society, where men are involved in different worlds each having a measure of autonomy, it will also be normal that a Christian belongs to more than one Christian congregation. This will be the implication of acknowledging that the congregation based on locality does not have priority over all the others. Yet the fact that the Church is a congregation and not a series of segregations must never be abandoned. This means that the structures of the Church and its ministry must be such that the unity of men in Christ, simply as human beings, is never hidden by the multiplicity of their involvements in the different communities in which their lives as Christians have to be lived. We recognize here, in the special terms of our secularized society, the same tension which we saw earlier in speaking of St Paul and Robert de Nobili, the tension between the obligation to take seriously the human communities in which men live, and within which they must hear and answer the call of God for obedience and his offer of reconciliation, and the obligation to take equally seriously the solidarity which is offered to all men simply as human beings, in Christ's atonement.

It is obvious that, in a secularized society, we cannot think of the Church as a place where directives are given about the way different sectors of the common life are to be ruled, directives which the individual Christian must try to carry out as he does his daily duty in the sector where he works. The Church will not be, in this sense, something over and above society. It will be the community of all men and women who are actually engaged in these several sectors of the common life, and who are together seeking to discover and demonstrate what God's will is for each of these sectors. It will be those who are thus involved in these areas of thought and life, who must make these discoveries. They will be themselves secular men who take seriously and have sought to master the technical factors and the guiding principles which are accepted as governing their work. But as Christians they will be living as a community of believers, who acknowledge Christ as Lord over all principles and powers, and who are constantly renewed by grace, freed from guilt and self-concern, liberated for the service of others, and eager to discern and follow the leading of the Spirit in the decisions which they have to make. If the Church in a secularized society is to answer to that description, it seems to me that these communities of Christians in particular sectors of the common life will have to be recognized as congregations of the Church of God, as truly as are the local congregations in the traditional forms of society from which we are emerging.

There is one element in the situation of the Church in the world about which I have so far said nothing, but which cannot be ignored. I have spoken all the time of the Church in the singular. What are we to say of the fact that the one Church of Jesus Christ is present in the world not as a single society, but as a fantastic medley of splintered fragments? Let me not add one more to the endless denunciations of our disunity which seem to move us so very little, and let me simply make this obvious point. I have said that mission is more than church extension. It is that daring act of self-emptying which mirrors and in a true sense re-enacts the self-emptying of the Son of God. It is the Christian going out, leaving familiar forms and words behind him, becoming a child who cannot speak till someone teaches him the alphabet, but believing that the God who raises the dead can take his nothingness and create out of it something new, a manifestation of the life of Jesus in the idiom of a new people and a new culture. If this be so, then it is a very parody of mission when divided churches go to a new people or a new community and seek to reproduce there their own divided existence. Go to the great new industrial complex of Durgapur in India, where thousands of Indians are being thrown together from every part of the country into the melting-pot of a new kind of society. Can you really try to turn them into Anglicans, or Methodists or Canadian Baptists or Danish Lutherans? Wherever you come from, and through whatever tradition you learned Christ, you have only one thing to do there: to empty yourself for Christ's sake in order humbly to learn what kind of a community can truly represent his intention for that industrial community. Only that can be worthy of the incarnation and the atonement. Only that contains the hope of resurrection. It would, of course, be possible to erect a series of fishing stations around that pool and fish for proselytes; but that is not mission. That will not create in Durgapur a community which is the first-fruit for Christ of the whole, an earnest of his purpose and a sign of his victory. Already the missionary experience of the past two centuries has helped powerfully to bring home to the Churches the scandal of their division. It is even more certain that a serious attempt at missionary penetration of the structures of a secularized society will make our divisions look ridiculous. I do not for a moment pretend that there are not real questions of truth at stake in our denominational differences. But they are very largely irrelevant to the questions we have to

answer when we try to interpret God's will for industry or
for public life. Effective mission in a secularized world will
require us to be ready to work together, to subdue the lust
for denominational dividend, to rejoice when Christ is
acknowledged and obeyed, whoever be the minister through
whom that obedience was wrought, to fall into the ground
and die in order that there may be fruit.

There is much that can be done in this direction even
short of full organic unity among the Churches. The slogan
JOINT ACTION FOR MISSION has been coined to describe
what can happen when the Churches are willing to recognize
a particular area, or a particular sector of the common life
as a mission field which must be seen as a whole and for
which the Churches must plan together for the sake of a
coherent and relevant witness to the purpose of God for
that nation, or city, or sector of the common life, without
seeking to create extensions or colonies of themselves in it.
The Indian industrial area of Durgapur, which I have
already mentioned, is one place where this is being at-
tempted. In Taiwan a plan is being developed at present
by the Churches to survey the total life of the island and
plan a total common Christian strategy for all parts of the
island and for all sectors of its life. Fifteen teams are at
present doing the research necessary to provide the basis for
a common strategy, and it is hoped that at the end of 1965
the Churches will be ready to embark together upon joint
action. Still another example has come to my personal
knowledge in the city of Wilmington, Delaware, a city
which was industrialized at a very early date and has in an
advanced form the typical problems of suburban development and inner city decay. The outskirts of the city contain
some of the wealthiest communities in the United States,
while the centre is a desolate area of slums, left to poor
whites, Negroes and Puerto Ricans. The Churches have
agreed to divide the whole city into a series of sectors in
each of which affluent suburban congregations participate as
equal partners with those in the inner city, and each of

which contains a representative selection of Churches – Lutheran, Methodist, Presbyterian, Episcopal and others. It has been agreed that these Churches will do their basic planning not as denominations, but in these sectors or larger parishes, so that everything will be done for the sake of the total service and witness given in the name of Christ to the city as a whole and not for the sake of denominational church extension. These are examples which happen to have come to my own knowledge of the sort of joint action for mission which is possible short of actual organic union. They express the intention of Christians who are taking seriously the secular character of modern society, that the Church shall be seen as the servant people going out to serve men in the specific needs of their several situations, the body which exists for all men, and not a specialized religious society competing with others for membership.

Such experiments, however, as those involved in them would be the first to agree, can only be pointers towards a fuller unity, and not a substitute for it. There can be no final escape from the truth that the Church, if it is to be the faithful witness of man's true end, must be recognizable in the world as one family, as a household in which men of every sort can be at home because it is the Father's house. It must find the forms of unity flexible enough to allow for the freedom of missionary experiment in all the different sectors of the human community, and yet strong enough to make variety a source of enrichment and not of conflict. The more seriously we take the missionary principle that Christians must be ready to go into every human situation, accepting that *kenosis* without which there cannot be a true incarnation of the life of Christ in a new community, the more necessary will it be that the bonds of unity are strong enough and flexible enough to hold all together.

I have spoken of the life of the Church in terms of the words 'come' and 'go'. The Church is indeed a gathering of those whom the Holy Spirit calls into the fellowship of

Christ. But it is never enough for the Church simply to be there and to say 'Come'. There has to be a movement of *kenosis*; one has to be willing to go, to become simply the unrecognized servant of men where they are, in order that *there*, perhaps in quite new forms, the authentic substance of the new life in Christ may take shape and become visible. It would be easy to speak of this as a rhythm, a double movement of going and coming in the life of the Church, and this would be true. But there is something more to be said. It is that in fact God himself scatters and gathers his Church. There are vivid examples of this in the recent history of missions. Fifty years ago the life of the Christian Church in many parts of Asia and Africa was chiefly visible in the form of gatherings of Christians around the mission stations with their schools and other institutions. Christians lived in communities under the care of a pastor or mission-ary. But many processes, including both the general process of secularization and also acts of deliberate government policy, are scattering these concentrations. Christians are to be found in ones and twos all over the place, as teachers, technicians, clerks, policemen, or in a hundred other jobs. Often they are in places where no church or mission has ever worked. Too often this has been viewed from the angle of a traditional settled community as an impossible pastoral problem. We mount our priests on motor-cycles and send them rushing around the country as peripatetic dispensers of sacraments. If we had a more biblical understanding of the Church we would see this not as a pastoral problem but as the great missionary opportunity that it is. We would find that these scattered Christians can quickly become the beginnings of new Christian congregations. The single Chris-tian technician in a new Government factory will find that there are others who want to come to his room at night to read the Scriptures with him. He becomes in a short time the centre of a group of believers. Only our stubborn adher-ence to conceptions of the ministry and of vocation derived from a different situation prevent us from seeing that God has in fact called this man to become the pastor of a new congregation, and that our business as stewards and not owners of the means of grace is to follow where the Spirit has led and authorize him by ordination to be what God has called him to be. One of the things which the process of secularization is doing everywhere is to break up old patterns of community, among them venerable Christian communities, and to scatter Christians in ones and twos throughout the manifold and varied sectors of a complex society, as well as to scatter a growing number of Christians all over the world in the service of technical development, government and education. If our doctrine of the Church is truly biblical we shall recognize that here the ancient pattern is reasserting itself. God is scattering in order that he may gather, as he did with the infant Church in Jerusalem when Herod put forth his hand to destroy it. When the fire is scattered, two things may happen: the scattered pieces may burn out, or they may start a wider conflagration. When the young Church was scattered abroad from Jerusalem this was what happened. It can happen again today. The condition is that Christians should remember that they are called to be a pilgrim people, to travel light, to leave behind, if necessary, much of the baggage accumulated during a long encampment, to follow without procrastination wherever the Spirit leads. For the promise of the Spirit is given only to those who go. And if the experience of one missionary is to be trusted, I would add that one has to run to keep up with him.

5 *Chap*

LIVING FOR GOD

IN THIS final chapter I want to look afresh, in the light of the preceding discussion, at the relation between religion and the secular and, more exactly, to ask what, for the Christian, is the role of religion in the life of a secular society.

There are at least three ways in which the opposition between religion and the secular is referred to in current Christian writing:

Firstly, a secular society is described as one in which the citizen is not subject to pressure from the state, or from the organs of society, to conform to a particular set of beliefs.

Secondly, a secular ethic is described as one which does not subordinate the actual concrete decision to an alleged supranatural law or standard, but permits it to be made on the basis of the empirical realities of the situation in each case.

Thirdly, a secular style of life for the Christian is described as one which does not turn away from the world to seek God, but finds God by involvement in the life of the world.

I hope that the discussion of these three issues will help us to make more precise distinctions, and to indicate the sense in which a Christian must still be a religious man and a secular man at the same time.

I

The Secular Society

On one point there is little dispute: we have left behind us the period of human history when Christianity was the established religion of the most powerful part of the human race. The Christendom era has ended. It can no longer be expected·that the Church will have the power of the state and the influence of society on its side. Attempts to restore that situation are doomed to failure. The world in the decades ahead of us will not be conformed to *The Idea of a Christian Society*,[1] in spite of the eloquent advocacy of T. S. Eliot, nor will it be controlled by the ideology of the 'four absolutes', in spite of the heroic labours of Moral Rearmament. Christian obedience calls for other kinds of response than these. Nor need Christians regret this. The 'Christendom Era' is not normative for the Church. It can be an exhilarating and liberating experience to be called to live as Christians in a situation nearer to that of the New Testament than to that of the nineteenth century.

But the end of 'Christendom' does not bring us back to the situation before Constantine. We have in fact to deal with four radically different situations. There is, first of all, the western part of the old Christendom, in all of which a basically secular society develops out of the former Christian establishment. The remnants of that establishment are still visible, sometimes impressive. The Church still makes itself seen and felt as a venerable and sometimes influential institution in education, broadcasting, social and personal services to the community, and on ceremonial public occasions. More important than these is the half-conscious but enormously powerful influence of Christian ethical teachings upon behaviour. If one doubts this, one must live for a time in Asia and then return to Europe. These western secular societies are a product of the Christendom era and inexplicable without it.

[1] London: Faber and Faber (1939).

In the second place, there are those parts of the former Christendom which are now parts of the communist world. Here also the Church is visible as an ancient and once venerable institution, but without the influence in public life which it can still exercise in the western world. Its role here is different. By its insistence on combining political loyalty to the régime with a stubborn refusal of the official ideology; by its continued witness through the life of worship to another reality beyond those recognized by the régime; by the simple fact of its continued existence as a distinct entity unabsorbed by the omnicompetent state; it introduces into the life of these societies what one may call a de-sacralizing principle. In some of the Marxist societies this witness of the Church is moving beyond silent protest to explicit dialogue welcomed on both sides.

In the third place, there are the 'new nations' of Asia and Africa, recently freed from the control of the European powers and seeking to develop a stable national life as independent entities. Here there is no background of 'Christendom' except as it was represented in the mission compounds and the colonial chaplaincies. The major impact of the western world has been through education (much of it initiated by Christian mission), through commercial and industrial development, and through the impact of political ideas. The Churches are small minorities, generally with little direct influence on the course of national life. While the power of the old religions in the life of society is diminishing, they still have an immense influence upon the way in which men think and act. The process of secularization is still, especially in the Islamic countries, in an early stage. The dominant problem is to find the foundations upon which a stable and coherent society can be built up, and to do so in the face of the accelerating population explosion and the growing pressure of hunger.

Finally, there is the People's Republic of China, constituting almost one-quarter of the human race, which cannot be included in any of the three groups already listed.

Here, in the area where the greatest single effort of western missionary expansion was concentrated, and where the Church is nevertheless an extremely small minority, the ancient sacral society has been replaced by a social order founded upon an apocalyptic and militant marxism. All the evidence suggests that the transformation here has been more rapid and more radical than in any other nation. There seems at present to be no evidence that this marxist society is undergoing the kind of 'de-sacralizing', the kind of movement towards a genuine secularity, which has been noted in speaking of the marxist societies of Eastern Europe.

This fourfold classification of the present human societies is obviously as rough and incomplete as any such classification must be. It leaves open the question whether the Latin American republics should be included in the first or the third group. My purpose in offering it is simply to remind the reader that when we embark upon a discussion of the secular state we must remember the great diversity of the human situation. Too much that is written takes the Western European and North American situation as normal, and founds analysis and argument upon a situation which is by no means that of the whole of the human race. Our discussion of the role of the Church in the process of secularization must be faithful to the total context.

Dr D. L. Munby in his book, *The Idea of a Secular Society*, argues the case for a positive Christian attitude towards the secular society, in opposition to the views of Mr T. S. Eliot, and lists the following as characteristics of the secular society.

((i) It 'refuses to commit itself as a whole to any particular view of the nature of the universe and of the place of man in it'. In such a society the views of atheists and of Christians will be equally respected, and will be given equal opportunity to influence education, broadcasting and other aspects of public life. Such a society will not accept the view of A. R. Vidler (following Gladstone) that the state has an obligation to acknowledge religious truth as well as to uphold ethical values, and will therefore not approve any state recognition of religion.

(ii) A secular society will be a pluralist society in the sense that it will not enforce (whether by social pressure or by state regulation) 'a uniform attitude in important matters of human behaviour and values'. It will thus accept the fact that education will 'be as much a sphere of divided beliefs and cultures as any other realm of life'.

(iii) A secular society will be a tolerant society. It will, certainly, act against beliefs which are 'in effect a form of activity directed against the accepted policies of society', but it will not accept the view of Sir Patrick Devlin that a general disgust at, for example, homosexuality is sufficient ground for society to take action against it. It is admitted that the line is very hard to draw here, but a stable secular society will give the benefit of the doubt to deviant belief and conduct.

(iv) The organizations and institutions of a secular society will have strictly limited aims. The aim of economic organization is to provide men with the widest possible variety of goods and services. The aim of political and judicial institutions is similarly limited. A secular society deflates the pretensions of politicians and judges to be leaders of society or 'prophet-priests of the national conscience'.

(v) A secular society will solve its problems by collecting and analysing the relevant facts so that people may be able to take rationally the decisions necessary to enable them to achieve their desires; it will not try to tell people what their desires ought to be.

(vi) A secular society will be a society without 'official images'. 'If there are no common aims, there cannot be a common set of images reflecting the common ideals and emotions of everyone. Nor can there be any common ideal types of behaviour for universal application.'[1]

[1] D. L. Munby, *The Idea of a Secular Society*, Oxford University Press (1963), pp. 14-31.

Dr Munby, in his book, is not describing any society which actually exists. The background of his discussion is Britain at the end of the Macmillan era. Certain things are therefore assumed which would not be present in a discussion in another context. It is a serious question how far these unstated assumptions invalidate the claim which Munby is making that the secular society which he sketches is the one towards which Christians ought to work. We may entirely agree with him in discarding any idea that the 'Christian Society' of T. S. Eliot can be established in twentieth-century Britain, but yet question whether he has assumed too easily the stability of society, the rationality and emotional coherence of the people about whom he is writing. Let me press this question briefly in relation to four elements in the life of society.

(*a*) *Politics.* A secular society, says Munby, will deflate the pretensions of politicians to be leaders of society and architects of manners and morals. Is this programme possible except in a society which has already achieved a high degree of stability? Is it possible that the new nations of Africa can overcome the centrifugal power of tribalism and evoke from their peoples the discipline, the sacrifice, and the integrity necessary for the realizing of their hopes for development if they do not have politicians who are 'leaders' in the sense which Munby deprecates? Granted the peril of false messianism, of the personality-cult in all its varied forms, and of the fascism which is always a near possibility, can politics be so completely de-sacralized as the ideal of a secular society requires? Would it be possible, for example, for such a thoroughly secular society as the Swiss Confederation to retain its solidarity if such a vast amount of trouble were not spent in school, and after it, to keep alive in the minds of all the people a sense of the historic events by which Switzerland has become what it is? Can even a moderately stable society like that of Britain endure indefinitely the process of 'deflation' without serious consequences?

Probably there is no generally applicable answer to these questions. But it is not necessary for our present purpose to answer them. What is surely important is to recognize that the idea of a secular society is not an idea that can stand by itself. A society can be truly secular, escaping the perils of messianism on the one hand, and of decay and dissolution on the other, if there are enough men and women in it who acknowledge an obligation to the common good which has deeper foundations than those of loyalty to a political leader or a political idea. These foundations are *religious* foundations. As Munby says towards the end of the lectures from which I have quoted, 'The secular world has its limited aims, and God respects these: there are no other alternative aims for Christians in their everyday life. But Christians, believing in God, can see these aims as *limited*, precisely because they look for *ultimate* satisfaction to God alone.'[1] Christians will be able to play their proper role in a secular society precisely in the measure in which they are rooted in a religious reality, in the knowledge of satisfactions which go beyond the aims of that society. And, conversely, the secular society will be able to endure, and to achieve its goals, in the measure in which it is served by men and women who have been delivered from the service of all false gods and messiahs for the service of the crucified and regnant Son of Man.

(b) *Law*. Equally, says Munby, the secular state will deflate the pretensions of judges, 'who vainly attempt to preserve some relics of their former role as prophet-priests of the national conscience'. What, exactly, is being proposed here? If judges in passing judgment are not called upon to give expression to the commonly held conviction of what is right and wrong, what is their business? What is their judgment other than the assertion of sheer power? Is it not the business of a judge to declare what is *just*, rather than what is expedient for those who are in power? Is the criminal

---

[1] Op. cit., p. 76.

simply the one who was unsuccessful? In other words, can any society endure in which no meaning remains to the phrase 'the majesty of the law'?

The sacral society is one in which there is a complete identification between the earthly lawgiver and the heavenly order. Against such a society the prophetic teaching of the Bible declares war. God alone is judge, and earthly judges are under his judgment and will be dethroned if they do not judge justly. The Bible, therefore, sanctions resistance to the established order of justice when it has become unjust. In that sense, the administration of justice is secularized; but only in that sense. Behind the earthly judge is the supreme judge. Those who acknowledge him will know both the truth of St Paul's statement that the powers that be are ordained by God, and also the truth of the prophetic attack upon the unjust judge. Without this *religious* acknowledgment of God as judge the secularization of human justice could only end in the total perversion of justice, where the proceedings of the law court are simply an integral part of the means by which the ruling group controls the rest.

(c) *Education*. By all odds this is the most sensitive and difficult area in which to apply the idea of a secular state to actual practice. A secular state, to quote Munby again, will not enforce 'a uniform attitude in respect of important matters of human behaviour and values'. It will be a society without common aims and therefore without official symbols in which these aims are expressed. However, it is not denied that there are matters of human behaviour and value which are 'important', even though views about them will differ. A large part of education consists in helping children to behave rightly and to judge rightly, and while this ought to lead to a kind of maturity which enables a man to live in a plural society and make his own decisions, that kind of maturity cannot be nourished in a school where no standards of behaviour are enforced and where there are no common aims. In regard to the various ideal pictures of the secular society, one is constantly forced to ask: what will they do in the schools?

I know of no answer to these questions which will be applicable to all situations. It seems to me that there may be situations where it is right for Christians to conduct their own schools, provided that equal rights are available to other groups to do the same. This is not necessarily[1] to relapse into mediaevalism. There may be other situations where the Church should concentrate on the training of teachers, and yet others where attention should be concentrated on the development of Christian teachers' associations in which current educational issues can be discussed. What seems to be quite impossible is to imagine that one can conduct a school in which there are no accepted convictions about behaviour and about values. To pretend to do so will merely be to be unaware of one's own convictions. A secular state will have to recognize this fact and therefore deliberately provide, as Munby suggests, for a variety of different kinds of schools in which different conceptions of what is a good education have freedom of expression. But there are, and there will surely always be, many societies which feel themselves unable to afford the luxury of this pluralism. The 'new' nations of Asia and Africa have, for understandable reasons, felt themselves compelled at an early stage to take a firm grip on the schools, because it was only in this way that they could hope to create the kind of unity of outlook necessary for national development. The danger is obvious, but it is not easy for relatively comfortable and stable societies to criticize this decision. In such situations the Churches may render their best service not by trying to create or preserve a separate system of church schools, but by training and equipping Christians to take their place in the national system. Within that system they will be able to exercise a genuinely secularizing function, and this may prove to be very necessary, in resisting the inevitable tendency to de-

[1] In spite of Harvey Cox, op. cit., p. 221.

velop a national ideology, in bearing witness constantly to the reality of things which lie beyond national political and economic goals. In this way Christian teachers in Africa during the next decade may have a vital role to play in resisting the tendency to look at education simply as a form of investment in national economic development. They may have a role in safeguarding the significance of the human person. But, once again, they will be able to perform this function only from a *religious* base, only on the basis of a life of worship, prayer and discipline which are rooted realities which transcend the immediate national programmes.

(*d*) *Economic Activity.* In a secular society, economic organization will have limited aims. It will not be frightened (says Munby) by Karl Marx's charge that capitalist society has replaced the idyllic relations of a former order with the cold callousness of a cash nexus. A secular society will regard economic organization, like all other forms of organization, as a strictly utilitarian arrangement for achieving a limited aim. To put right the admitted defects we do not need a new economic system. We just have to pull ourselves together and behave properly. 'If we allow these powers (of modern science) to be misused, we are ourselves to blame.' The ideal of a secular economic organization will be that all jobs have equal status, and this ideal 'merely requires that men should not think more highly of themselves and of their social and economic position than they think of that of others, and that they should not look up to others with awe and respect merely because of their position'. Economic activity in a secular society is a big job of team work, calling for sound organization. Secular man, as Cox describes him in his attractive delineation of this aspect of 'The Secular City',[1] does not need Augustine's God, Adam Smith's invisible hand, or Karl Marx's dialectic; he organizes a research team to isolate and solve the immediate problem, and then reorganizes his work team to do the job. He does

[1] Op. cit., p. 69.

not feel any need to relate everything to some ultimate world-view.

Munby is less than fair to himself when he says that the secular ideal of economic organization 'merely' requires that men should not think too highly of themselves: his continuing argument shows how tough we must expect the struggle to be between competing groups in a modern economic system. One can accept as true the sketch which is given of the economic aspects of a secular society, and yet feel bound to insist that the toughest question has been left untouched. There is evidence to suggest that the whole modern concept of 'organization' as distinct from the earlier conception of 'order' is rooted in the biblical demand for personal decision vis-à-vis the coming of the Kingdom of God.[1] Whether this is true or not, organization is impossible without a highly developed sense of personal responsibility. At a more primitive stage capitalist economies depended upon recurrent periods of deflation and unemployment to ensure a powerful motivation both for workers and for entrepreneurs to remain at the highest possible level of efficiency, however inefficient the system as a whole might be. Modern techniques of control have eliminated the necessity for these recurrent catastrophes. The problem of economic motivation has become a pressing one. A system can continue running for a long time on motivations which have been inherited from a previous period, either a built-in fear of poverty, or a religious sense of the obligation to work hard, or a combination of the two. But this cannot continue indefinitely. The more highly rational an economic system becomes, the more this question will be posed. It is difficult to see how, in a rationally organized welfare state in which all the techniques of planning now available are used effectively, the question of motivation can be evaded. It is possible that it may be answered by means of some sort of ideological pressure upon the individual. As André Dumas has said, ideologies are the source of wars, tortures, terror-

[1] D. von Oppen, quoted by Cox, op. cit., pp. 177ff.

isms of all kinds, but 'they have also been, and still are.
the great moral force of the contemporary masses'. Professor
Dumas goes on: 'One of the pressing problems today is
that of moral impetus when ideologies lose their power and
crumble. Does not our lucid decompression risk leading man
to the sole pursuit of his own possessive and deaf "little bit
of happiness"?'[1] Where, without ideology, shall the secular
economic order find the roots of that sense of personal
responsibility for the other without which organization
cannot function? Can it be (again, I repeat, leaving aside
both the survival of sentiments derived from a former era,
and the possibilities of a new ideology) – can it be otherwise
than in a *religious* sense of responsibility towards the one
who has loved us and bidden us love our brother? Can a
truly secular economic order survive the disappearance of a
religious motivation?

In putting these questions, let me repeat, I am not
trying to prepare the way for a reassertion of the idea of
a Christian society. I do not think that Christians should
be trying either to preserve or to restore the 'Christendom'
situation. I can express my concern positively in a twofold
way.

Firstly, the secular society is conceivable only if religion
continues to be a living reality. Secularity is not by itself
enough to sustain a human society in being. At this point
I would like to make a reference which may seem surprising
in the present context. Those who seek for a secular reinterpretation of the Gospel are apt to regard pietism as
one of the enemies. But the rise of pietism was surely a
tremendously important element in the process by which
the way was prepared for the idea of a secular society.
Pietism broke with the conception of the *corpus christianum*. It made a distinction between membership in the
'sacral' society of Christendom and a living personal relationship with Jesus Christ. It thereby laid the foundations
both for the modern missionary movement, and for the

[1] *The Student World*, 1964, No. 3, pp. 257-8.

development of all kinds of Christian social action. At its best, it nurtured men and women in whom a deep personal religion issued in an active involvement in all kinds of public responsibility. At the present time pietism is often identified with a kind of religion which limits Christian obedience to a very narrow range of personal and domestic relationships, and is blind to the ethical issues raised by the new possibilities of human control over great areas of experience which were previously outside the reach of such control. This limited pietist ethic is quite unworthy of the Bible, with its unqualified assertion of the lordship of Christ over all things. It is rightly repudiated by those who are sensitive to the new ethical issues raised by the new human situation. But what needs to be repudiated is not the authentic substance of pietism, but its quite unnecessary stultification by a failure to recognize a new situation. The more one explores the idea of a secular society, the more clear does it become that such a society could be maintained only by the participation of men and women in whom commitment to Christ is a living, personal, religious reality. This is not to ask for the reconstruction of the sort of metaphysical 'world view' which secular man repudiates. It is to recognize that it is, in the last resort, only through the personal approach of the living God in Christ, and the response of men to him in living faith, that there can be nurtured and sustained those insights and those motivations without which a truly secular society cannot endure.

Secondly, and more fundamentally, I want to express the conviction that the idea of a secular society can only be rightly understood in the context of a biblical understanding of history. It cannot, if I may put it so, be rightly understood as if it were a timeless idea, a sort of blue-print for human society which, if it were adopted, would thenceforth provide the ideal conditions for human living. It can only be rightly understood in a historical perspective, in the light of the worldwide process which I tried to sketch at the beginning of this book, in the light of the different human situations in different areas of the world, and the light of the worldwide mission of the Church. The worldwide movement of secularization, of which we are a part, is, as the Mexico meeting[1] tried to say, a movement which holds out both negative and positive possibilities. At the same time breaking down ancient sacral structures by which men's lives have been controlled in the past, and putting into men's hands great new powers for the control of their world, it vastly increases the range of choice open to men, and draws them into a movement which may lead either to greater freedom or to new enslavement. A Christian, seeking to understand what is happening in the world from the point of view of the revelation of God in Jesus Christ, must recognize here the working out of God's purpose, revealed in Christ, to call men into the freedom where they can know him as their Lord. By the process of secularization men are prised loose from the control of traditional religious beliefs and moral standards and are compelled to make decisions where before everything was decided for them. We are right to see in this part of God's calling of mankind to maturity. But the New Testament gives us no ground for expecting that mankind as a whole will accept that calling. On the contrary, it suggests a deepening conflict between him who has come to set men free and the false messiahs who enslave men. From a theological point of view, therefore, the Christian will see the struggle to make and keep society secular as part of his obedience to God who wills to preserve for men an area of freedom in which they may accept their calling in Christ, in obedience to whom alone is perfect freedom. To imagine that secularity can, so to speak, stand alone, would be to fall into an ideology which would end by enslaving men.

One implication of this remains to be stated. It is that the proper Christian response to the process of secularization must include commitment to the world missionary task. I

[1] Conference on the Christian world mission held by the World Council of Churches in Mexico City in December 1963.

find this element lacking in many current discussions of the issue, the great exception being the book of van Leeuwen. Secularization, as van Leeuwen interprets it, is the present revolutionary phase of the impact of the biblical message upon mankind. It is a process which puts men in the situation of having to make new decisions, upon which depend the possibilities of freedom or bondage. The Christian Church in every land is called to the task of being witness to what God is doing in this worldwide process, so that those who are being drawn out of their traditional securities into this new and perplexing freedom may be helped to understand this experience as what it truly is, a calling to new responsibility before the Lord of history. I said at the beginning that the Christian missionary, whether he realizes it or not, has been an agent of secularization in the great non-western cultures. The corollary of that has now to be stated. The task of the missionary who goes from the western world at the call of the churches of Asia and Africa to preach the Gospel, will be to be the interpreter who stands at the point where secularization is cutting into the ancient way of life, making clear by his word and his manner of life the way in which a Christian can accept the offer of freedom which secularization brings. It has been rightly said that, while the Church has some successes to its credit in its effort to develop truly indigenous forms within the old cultures of Asia and Africa, it has conspicuously failed to develop forms which are 'at home' on the frontier between the old and the new, the frontier on which more and more of the peoples of these continents are called to live. In too many places the Church has succeeded in identifying itself with a culture which is disappearing. A truly biblical understanding of the process of secularization will lead the Church out to the frontiers where that process is most vigorously at work, to be the interpreter of the offer of freedom and of the threat of bondage which are hidden within the movement of secularization.

II

Ethics in a Secular Context

The process of secularization necessarily involves the questioning of accepted patterns of behaviour. In a sacral type of society these patterns are regarded as part of the ultimate constitution of things, bound up with the final realities which cannot be questioned. Secularization destroys these certainties and puts men in a position where they have to make conscious decisions about matters which were formerly taken for granted. This imposes heavy strains upon the individual. No society can exist without some accepted patterns of behaviour. It would be impossible to live in a society where the behaviour of one's neighbours was wholly unpredictable. Nor could one endure the strain of having to live without the support and guidance for oneself of generally accepted patterns of conduct. The breaking-up of these patterns by the process of secularization is both an opportunity for new freedom and also an occasion for new strains upon the human spirit.

The continuity of the process of secularization with the biblical story of God's breaking into history in Christ is especially clear at this point. One of the remarkable things about St Paul's treatment of the law in his writings is that, at certain points, he includes it among the powers which have held men in bondage and which Christ has dethroned by the victory of his cross and resurrection. Hendrikus Berkhof, in his book *Christ and the Powers*, has shown how Paul understands the 'Powers' as, on the one hand, 'the framework of creation, preserving it from disintegration . . . the dyke which prevents the chaotic deluge from submerging the world'; and, on the other hand, as that which stands between us and the life of freedom as children of God. They are the framework which prevents a world without Christ from disintegrating; but in Christ they are robbed of their absolute power over men. In the famous passage Colossians 2.13-15, this is specifically applied to the 'ordinances' of the law, and in such a way as to make it clear that it applies both to Jewish and to Gentile regulations which purported to govern human life. The regulations have indeed performed a necessary function in preserving human society from chaos. They are part of God's provision for humanity. But in Christ their false claim to absolute power is unmasked. They are not absolutes, not the ultimate guarantee of human happiness and godliness. Now that Very God himself has appeared on earth, it is found that they have acted not as his instruments but as his enemies. To quote Berkhof, 'The scribes, representatives of the Jewish law, crucified him in the name of the law. The priests, servants of the temple, crucified him in the name of the temple. The pharisees, personifying piety, crucified him in the name of piety. Pilate, representing Roman justice and law, showed what these are worth when called upon to do justice to the Truth himself.'[1] Christ has thus, in his Cross, unmasked the 'powers', making a public spectacle of them. To those who have seen this, they are no longer absolutes. The only absolute is the living Christ himself, and the only true life is a continual participation in this life of Christ. To go back to the control of the 'powers', to rules and regulations of all sorts, is to go back from freedom into slavery. The Colossians had to be warned against just this danger.

The process of secularization is the continuation of this process of unmasking, of dethronement. It is obvious that this takes place far beyond the sphere in which the Gospel is actually preached and heard. The work of the Christian doctor in Asia and Africa was very often the means of the visible dethronement of the ancient powers, as was also the work of the Christian school in India which deliberately broke the ancient laws of caste. Today the same process continues with accelerated speed in the work of secular medicine and education. But this process opens the way to two different possibilities. It can lead on the one hand to a

[1] H. Berkhof, op. cit., p. 31.

new life of freedom in Christ. This new life is described over and over again by St Paul in terms of dying with Christ in order to live with him. It is a life in which all the defences that man erects against God, even the defence of his ethics and his religion, is swept away and he learns to live in a simple and childlike dependence on the love of his Father. It is a life in which every kind of self-justification has been ruled out in favour of one simple intention – to pay back the unpayable debt of gratitude to Christ by giving oneself to one's neighbour. It is a life in which the impossible commandment to love one's neighbour as oneself has become possible because it is no longer a commandment but a gift.

The other possibility is that the dethroning of the old absolutes opens the flood-gates to chaos in which men are simply lost until some new pseudo-absolute emerges to impose some sort of order. But this is in fact a pseudo-order. It has not, though it seeks to clothe itself with, the authority of the old 'sacral' order. The process of secularization is, in this respect, irreversible. The power of these pseudo-orders is brittle; the lies which they are bound to use in order to remain in being destroy their claims to authority.

The Christian has no interest in trying to re-establish the 'absolutes' which have been dethroned by the process of secularization. But neither should he be under any illusions about the impossibility of human life without any guidance from accepted patterns of conduct. This is not a matter of kindly accommodation to the needs of those who do not have personal knowledge of the life of freedom in Christ. For the Christian, also, such patterns are necessary. The letters of St Paul are our best guides at this point. On the one hand, they leave no room for a life which is 'under the law'. They show how Christ has demolished the pretensions of the law to be able to bring men to God, and how the man in Christ is liberated from bondage to the law in order to live a life of freedom – the life of an adult person in the

Father's house, a life led by the Spirit and not controlled by a legal code. The whole of the law, says St Paul, is summed up in a single command: love your neighbour as you love yourself.

But, on the other hand, the Apostle does not simply leave the matter there. He recognizes that the question must inevitably be asked: what kind of conduct does love require? He does not dismiss this as an unnecessary question. He is not content to leave his readers simply with the instruction: love, and do what you will.

Two features characterize his answers to the question of conduct. In the first place, they are largely drawn from the current ethical teaching of his time. It has been shown that there are many parallels between the ethical sections of the Epistles and the popular lists of ethical advice current in the world to which Paul and his readers belonged. This is a point worth noting. The Christian's conduct is not simply deduced from timeless truths. It takes seriously the accepted patterns of each time and place. This means that there will be different patterns of conduct for Christians in different times and places. This is in turn rooted to the fact that the Christian's life is understood in a historical perspective – understood, that is to say, from the point of view of its place in the carrying to completion of God's purpose for the whole life of mankind.

But, in the second place, these patterns of behaviour are not imposed upon the believer as laws. Rather they are hints, reminders, of the kind of behaviour to which love of one's neighbour will lead in the concrete circumstances of the time and place where one lives. They do not become a new law. St Paul never suggests that it is by keeping on the right side of the lines which he sketches that his readers will find salvation and peace with God. The logic is quite different. The Christian has been given salvation and peace with God as a totally undeserved gift. He cannot earn it. He does not have to work for it. It has been given. His whole duty is to make his life an act of free and joyful thanksgiving. These lines of conduct are suggested as hints to guide him. They are not the absolutes by which he directs his life. The only absolute is Christ himself, Christ crucified, risen and present. It is by reference to him, to his great acts of love and grace, that the Christian is moved and guided. All else has a secondary place – secondary, but not unnecessary.

This well-known character of St Paul's teaching on the Christian life is very important for understanding the ethical problems posed by the process of secularization. In discussion of these problems it is too common to hear 'religion' opposed to 'secular ethics' in terms which simply identify 'religion' with what Paul calls 'the law'. This seems to me to be one of the weaknesses of Mr John Wren-Lewis's discussion of these questions. If a 'religious' ethic means an ethic of sheer blind submission to external standards of behaviour supposed to belong to a supra-natural order of being, then the Christian must be against it. This means, for example, that the attempt to deduce a binding law on the subject of divorce from the recorded teaching of Jesus rests on a wrong understanding of the nature of the Christian life. But in accepting the secularist's rejection of *this* kind of supra-naturalist ethic, we must decline to agree that the Christian is not concerned with supra-natural realities in his ethical decisions. The Christian life is nothing at all if it is not a continuous response to the living Lord himself, the one who has manifested the mind of God towards us, who has died for us and risen again for us, who lives to make intercession for us, who summons us to find life in living for him. The Christian life is a life rooted in a religious relation to Christ – not the religion of bondage to law, but the religion of free worship and obedience in the Spirit. This becomes clear in the fact that in his appeals to his readers St Paul repeatedly brings the most tremendous supernatural realities to bear upon the solution of the most ordinary ethical problems. In asking his friends to live in unity he invokes as the ground of his appeal the self-emptying of

Christ in his incarnation. As the basis of his advice to
married couples he speaks of the marriage of Christ and
the Church. This is a supra-naturalist ethic indeed! But it
is not a legalist ethic. It is wholly concerned with, based
upon, directed to the revealed will of him who made us,
who redeemed us, and who will at the end be our judge.

In all our ethical decisions we have to do with him. We
are not *just* concerned with the situation, though it is only
in the concrete situation that we can meet him in obedience
or disobedience. Not any supposed eternal laws or principles, but he, the living Lord, is the one with whom we
have to reckon. And he cannot be mocked. This means that
there is a negative word to be spoken also. There are ways
of behaving which exclude the possibility of fellowship
with God. The apostle is quite blunt about this. 'I warn
you, as I warned you before, that those who behave in such
ways will never inherit the Kingdom of God' (Gal. 5.21).
This negative word must be heeded. If God is as Jesus has
revealed him, then certain kinds of behaviour must lead to
death, even though they may be generally accepted in the
society to which we belong. At this point the supra-naturalist
character of the Christian ethic becomes sharply apparent.
It speaks of a word from beyond the *mores* of society:
'Thou shalt not . . .'.

This negative statement of the Christian ethic is often
criticized just because it is negative. It is true that a life
dominated by these negatives is sterile. Only love is the
fulfilment of the law, and love is wholly positive. Nevertheless, to admit this is not to deny the validity of the other in
its proper place. The negatives fence off an area wherein
we have the freedom to learn what love means. They mark
the edges of the road we have to travel. They are like the
fence which protects the traveller from falling over the edge
into the ravine below. It is not a sign of maturity but of
folly to seek to destroy the fence. Nor is it the mark of an
adult to see how near he can go to the edge without falling
over. The question: 'How much is allowed?' is the typical

question of the child. The adult question is: 'What is worth
having? What journey is worth making? What goal is worth
reaching?' When that question is answered, the adult man
knows that there is a discipline to be accepted if he is to
reach the goal he has chosen. He will know that he cannot
reach the goal unless he keeps to the way.

St Paul therefore describes the Christian life in the language of an athlete. There is a goal to be reached, a prize
to be won. It is the one supremely worthwhile object of a
man's desire. The wise man will cheerfully accept whatever
discipline is needed for reaching it. 'You know,' says the
Apostle, 'that in the sports all the runners run the race,
though only one wins the prize. Like them, run to win. But
every athlete goes into strict training. They do it to win a
fading wreath; we, a wreath that never fades' (I Cor. 9.24-
25). And in another passage he speaks of his life as 'pressing towards the goal to win the prize which is God's call
to the life above' (Phil. 3.14).

These passages show the true place of religion in the
ethical life of a Christian. There is no trace of bondage
here to alleged supra-natural standards, to 'absolutes'. In
the very passage which we have quoted from the Corinthian
letter, where Paul describes his life in the language of
athletics, he shows with what complete freedom he deals
with the differing ethical standards of his time. He says
that he became a Jew to the Jews and a pagan to the pagans.
'I have become everything in turn to men of every sort.'
He is the completely secular man who knows the variety of
human patterns of behaviour and knows that none of them
is absolute. But in all this he is not behaving aimlessly. He
has a very clear aim. It is that he and those with whom
he has to do may be 'saved'—that is to say, may share in
the glory and the joy of God's completed work in Jesus
Christ.

This combination of freedom and discipline will be the
mark of a truly Christian life. It will have on the one hand
the freedom which is the mark of true secularity, freedom

from the tyranny of any particular pattern or code of behaviour, freedom to learn in every new situation what love
requires; and, on the other hand, the discipline without
which this freedom becomes an aimless and ultimately disastrous wandering. Both the freedom and the discipline are
rooted in a religious relation to the living Christ. The freedom is that which is made possible because Christ in his
dying and rising has de-throned the 'powers', broken the en-
tail of sin and guilt and death, and opened up the possibility
of a life of sonship. The discipline is wholly directed to him,
the living Christ. It consists, as Paul makes clear in the
Philippian passage, in an absolutely single-minded attention
to Christ himself. 'All I care for is to know Christ, to experience the power of his resurrection, and to share his
sufferings, in growing conformity with his death, if only I
may finally arrive at the resurrection from the dead.' The
religion of a Christian man will be exactly the discipline by
which he is enabled to do 'this one thing', and this religious
relation to the living Lord will be the inner substance of his
secular freedom, without which it will end in mere conformity to a dying world.

The fact of secularization, rightly understood, means that *devotions*
the ethical behaviour of the Christian will be more, and not
less, deeply rooted in a religious discipline. This has been
admirably stated by Professor André Dumas in the article
already quoted: 'Along with the disappearance of an ethic *is*
of Christendom should go the establishment of a clearly
christological ethic. Free play in the secular requires the
deepening of roots in the sacred, or rather in the revealed.
It is normal that Bonhoeffer, the Protestant ethical thinker
who best realized the new dimensions of faith and morals
in a world without religion, should also be the one who most
insisted on the personal character of obedience, of the
"following" (*Nachfolge*) of Jesus Christ.'[1] This following,
as Bonhoeffer expounds it in his *Ethics*, is not simply the
imitatio Christi. It is not a matter of 'trying to be like Jesus'.

[1] A. Dumas, *The Student World*, No. 3, 1964, p. 257.

It is a matter of allowing Christ to conform us to himself, the incarnate, crucified and risen one.[1] It is a matter of living in the faith that 'our life is outside ourselves and in Jesus Christ.'[2] It is, in short, what St Paul is speaking about in the passage which we have quoted from the Philippian letter.

But with this we are beginning to speak of the Christian's life of communion with God through Jesus Christ, and on this subject something must be briefly said.

III

Communion with God

Those who are seeking to restate the Christian message for a secularized society speak very frequently of the need for a kind of discipleship which is above all involved in the life of the world. 'Involvement' is now almost the primary virtue. By contrast the word 'religion' is tacitly identified with an activity which turns away from the world, abandoning it in favour of another realm where alone satisfaction is to be found. Traditional language about prayer and worship is suspect, lest it prove to be an escape from the real business of Christian living. The Church is held to be at its best when it is a filling station for the next lap of the course, and private prayer is seen as a sort of gathering together of the faculties for the next encounter with the world.

Let it be repeated that there are good reasons for this suspicion of 'religion'. There is plenty of religion in the world which is indeed an escape from reality, and the pagan heart of man, in all ages and places, has always a tendency to hanker after it. The fact that an activity is religious, is pious in the sense of the great traditions of human religion,

---

[1] Dietrich Bonhoeffer, *Ethics*, London: SCM Press (1955) (Collins, Fontana edition. pp. 80-1); New York: Macmillan.
[2] Op. cit., p. 218.

by no means guarantees that it is concerned with reality. Religious practice can be the place where our escape from reality, our hypocrisy and our sheer selfishness are at their maximum.

But what matters is the standpoint from which our criticism of religion is mounted. 'The world' is not a tenable standpoint. The only possible standpoint is that of faith in Christ, in whom alone both God and the world are made known as they are. Here Dietrich Bonhoeffer has said the decisive word: 'A life in genuine worldliness is possible only through the proclamation of Christ crucified; true worldly living is not possible or real in contradiction to the proclamation or side by side with it, that is to say in any kind of autonomy of the secular sphere; it is possible and real only "in, with the under" the proclamation of Christ.'[1] It is only in the presence of Christ, the incarnate, crucified and risen Lord, that we can speak truly about the world or be truly involved in it. In and through Christ alone do we know the world as it truly is, created in God's love, alienated from God's love, redeemed and renewed by God's love. True Christian involvement in the world is a life lived in the world in responsibility to him who is its Lord, and this responsibility means responding to him who has first acted, answering him who has first spoken, loving him who has first loved. It is responsibility to *him* who alone is worthy of our total self-giving. Without this supernatural reference, the programme of 'involvement' can only become that conformity to the world which is death. In pagan terms, the antithesis 'sacred' and 'worldly' may be valid. But in these terms, neither the world nor God is known. The only standpoint given to us from which we may know both God and the world, the only basis, therefore, for a true criticism of religion, is Jesus Christ the incarnate, crucified and risen Lord, in whom, as St Paul says, 'the world has been crucified to me, and I to the world'. In Christ the Christian learns both to deny and to affirm the world – to deny it in its self-

[1] *Ethics*, Fontana edition, p. 297.

sufficiency, to affirm it as the object of God's love. But this paradoxical unity of denial and affirmation is only possible from within a relationship of responsibility to him who is not of the world, to the Lord whose the world is because he is its creator and its redeemer. Apart from this communion with God, talk of holy worldliness will become utterly shallow.

The communion of the Christian with God is centred in the corporate worship of the Christian community, in which Christ's redeeming work is set forth in word and sacrament, and the believing community responds in worship, prayer, and oblation. In one sense this Christian worship might be described as a secular, this-worldly affair. Speaking, washing, eating, drinking – all these are secular activities. What is offered in worship is the ordinary life of the community, its daily work and its worldly wealth. But 'in, with and under' these things, the Christian is brought to the place where he offers what he can offer to no human being and to no secular institution – the unconditional surrender of his will and the unlimited adoration of his heart and mind. The meaning of Christian worship is set before us once and for all in the vision of the Apocalypse where the events of the secular world in which the seer lives are seen in the setting of the worship of the whole creation, of the throne of God set in heaven surrounded by a sea of glass like crystal, of a glory and majesty before which he can only fall prostrate in utter adoration. This worship of the living God, of him who sits upon the throne, of the Lamb slain standing in the midst of the throne, is the very centre of the Christian life. A pattern of discipleship from which it had been removed would not be in any recognizable sense Christian.

But, let it be said again, this worship of the living God as he has made himself known to us in Christ must be guarded against assimilation to pagan ways of worship which deny the reality of the incarnation and the atonement. Worship

which draws men's minds away from concern with the doing
of God's will in the world into an exclusive concern for the
blessedness of the worshippers is pagan worship. It must be
denounced in the name of the incarnate Lord. Christian
worship does not direct our thoughts *away* from the world;
it directs them to him who has come *to* the world. The very
heart of it is the act of humble and thankful adoration of
him who 'for us men and for our salvation came down from
heaven . . .'. It is in that act of divine grace that Christian
worship finds its focus of attention, and it is precisely that
act which gives the world its value. If we have to reject a
pagan conception of worship which draws men's thoughts
away from the world, we must also reject a formulation of
Christian belief, and consequently a conception of Christian
worship which removes attention from that act of God, that
mighty deed done for us by one who is not ourselves but
Another. It is just in that otherness, in that divine transcen-
dance (if we must use such language), without which it
would be meaningless to say 'God so loved the world . . .'
that there lies both the motive for Christian worship, and
the safeguard against a worship which tries to escape from
the world. If we were wholly robbed of *that* assurance of
the transcendant, if we were really to try to direct worship
to 'the ground of our being', apart from the faith that he
who is the ground of our being is also he who came for us,
died for us, rose for us and calls us into his fellowship, then
indeed we should be on the road to paganism.

This may seem a harsh word, but I think it is justified
by the way in which the subject of prayer is handled in
some of the recent restatements of the Christian faith for
secular men. If one thing is clear about the teaching and
practice of Jesus, it is that prayer was a profound reality for
him and that he expected it to be such for his followers.
And in the teaching of Jesus prayer is not a conversation
with oneself. It is not a soliloquy. It is not meditation in the
sense in which pagan religion is accustomed to that exercise.
It is an activity which involves two parties, the one who

prays and the one to whom prayer is addressed. It is the child talking to the Father, asking him for what is needed, thanking him for what he is and has done, trusting him to do what is good. It is possible because the Father has revealed himself as one who loves men to the uttermost. This love of God, this accessibility to the petitions of his children, is not something discovered from a study of the world, or deducible from the nature of man. It is revealed in his acts. The response to the revelation includes believing prayer, and the more a man is committed to doing the will of God in the world, the more he will know the need to pray. Indeed he will know that the deepest meaning of his deeds is simply that they are, to use Schweitzer's phrase, acted prayers for the coming of God's kingdom. Anyone who knows what it is to live a life of responsible action in the world, praying each day for the doing of God's will, asking boldly for what is needed for each day's tasks, looking eagerly for the answers to his prayers, and, in Bonhoeffer's phrase, 'delivering up himself and his deed to God'[1] each day, one who knows the adventure of this living discipleship – a man, in short, who knows what it is to trust the promises of the Gospel in this matter, will certainly not accept in its place the monologue of communion with himself. Prayer in the name and the spirit of Jesus, prayer patterned on his prayer, is no escape from the work of the world. It is the living heart of responsible dealing with the world.

All Christian thinking about communion with God comes to a focus in that act by which, both in word and in sacrament, the deed of God in Jesus Christ is set forth so that men may become not merely spectators of it, or reporters of it, but participants in it. Here the believing community returns week by week to the one place where God and the world are known as they truly are. Here the living God meets us, not as one who would draw us away from the world, but as one who has given himself for the life of the

[1] Op. cit., p. 253.

world. Here the double word is spoken – denial of the world
and affirmation of the world. Denial, in that Christ is set
forth crucified; in him the contradiction between God and
the world is made manifest and the judgment of God upon
the world is pronounced. Affirmation, in that Christ's victory
over the world is announced, new birth for the world is
made possible, new hope for the world is assured. In this
action we are not merely hearers of a proclamation, or
merely spectators of a transaction done for us. We are, by
Christ's own invitation and ordinance, made participants
in it. As we obey his commands – 'Take, eat, this is my
body'; 'This is my blood of the new covenant. Drink ye all
of it', we are ourselves drawn into this action of God. We,
the believing community, are made participants with Jesus
in his dying and rising. We know ourselves with all mankind
under God's judgment, and we know ourselves with all men
the objects of his love. In Christ we are offered up to the
Father with the whole life of mankind and with the whole
created world. We are made sharers in Christ's royal priesthood for the whole life of the world. We are sent out to
exercise that priesthood in the world. We are not sent out in
order to live united with God apart from the world, but to
live as the sign and first-fruit of God's uniting of the world to
himself in Christ. 'The Church' (to quote Bonhoeffer again)
'is nothing but a section of humanity in which Christ has
taken form.'[1] It can be this, only because at its centre there
is a place where, in the word and sacraments of the Gospel,
he himself can lay hold upon us so that we may be not conformed to this world but transformed by the renewing of
our minds.

This constantly renewed communion of the Christian
community with God is the heart of what Christians have
been accustomed to call their religion. We cannot accept the
wholly arbitrary confinement of the word 'religion' to that
sort of turning away from the world which is characteristic
of certain forms of paganism. In truth, the man who does

[1] Op. cit., p. 83.

not know Christ has good reason to turn away from the world and search for something better. It is the glory of the Christian Gospel that it speaks of one who is not of the world, who is all glorious and all gracious, as the world is not, but who so loved the world that he poured himself out to the uttermost so that the world might be full of his glory. It is because of the might and the grace of that immortal lover that the Christian, caught up in his love, can learn to love the world. It is through him who is not of the world that the Christian can learn to know and love the world.

But the last word is not of our learning, but of Christ's work in us. The heart of the matter is to be found in his prayer for his apostles on the night of his passion:

> I do not pray that thou shouldst take them out of the world, but that thou shouldst keep them from the evil one. They are not of the world even as I am not of the world. Sanctify them in the truth; thy word is truth. As thou didst send me into the world, so I have sent them into the world. And for their sake I consecrate myself, that they also may be consecrated in truth.

True religion for secular man is the abiding in that consecration.

INDEXES

INDEX OF NAMES

INDEX OF SUBJECTS

57-2

21 - 23 on history. (Sermons) 12 - ff. a new view of history 14 19-20

8 secular vs secularism defined

9 - his view on 'religion'. gospel is end of it, as of law.

24 - chr Se.

35 cf Marxism

37 generation of youth protestors insight

44 - ff. Election to historical responsibility

44 -- ct God in history, 47-8, 51

73 ff. conversion

83 - ff. faith : science - knowledge (79-81) and know by faith. Jn. 8

89 ✗ Repentance ? Confession

140 - ff Ethics + Paul ✗